Your Child's Unique

TEMPERAMENT

Insights and Strategies for Responsive Parenting

Sandee Graham McClowry

Research Press • 2612 North Mattis Avenue • Champaign, Illinois 61822
(800) 519-2707 • www.researchpress.com

Copyright © 2003 by Sandee Graham McClowry

5 4 3 2 1   03 04 05 06 07

Copies of this book may be ordered from Research Press at the address given on the title page.

Composition by Jeff Helgesen
Cover design by Linda Brown, Positive I.D. Graphic Design, Inc.
Printed by Bang Printing

ISBN 0–87822–491–2
Library of Congress Control Number 2003106132

To my children, Allison and Sean, who were patient with me
while I learned to be their mother

Contents

Figures and Tables

FIGURES

TABLES

Preface

The content presented in this book is based on the INSIGHTS into Children's Temperament program, conducted in a number of public schools in New York City. The program has had a long evolution and is fundamentally rooted in the multiple research studies I have conducted and in my clinical practice.

Several years ago, I conducted a study of middle-class Caucasian families whose children attended school in regular (not special-education) classrooms (McClowry et al., 1994). I selected this particular population because I wanted to contrast these families with a high-risk sample that was socioeconomically disadvantaged. My erroneous assumption was that the middle-class families would have few psychological problems. Instead, I found that, among the middle-class families that I considered a low-risk group, 25 percent of the children demonstrated a need for behavioral intervention, and one third of their mothers expressed significant levels of psychological distress. Moreover, the children's temperament strongly influenced whether the children were having behavior problems and the type of problems they exhibited. The children's behavior was further exacerbated if their mothers reacted strongly to their own daily hassles.

The need for services for families dealing with child behavior problems was evident. A number of behavioral interventions already existed, but nearly none of them took a child's temperament (a topic about which you will soon learn a great deal) into consideration. For more than a decade, I continued to study children's temperament. With the collaboration of experienced clinicians like Pamela Galehouse, I also piloted, and re-piloted, and re-piloted, again an intervention that eventually became known as INSIGHTS into Children's Temperament.

In 1998, the National Institute of Nursing Research awarded my research team $3.2 million to conduct a clinical trial to test the effectiveness of INSIGHTS in several New York City elementary schools. The families engaged in the study were, for the most part, high-risk families. Consequently, a comprehensive intervention was implemented. Parents and teachers attended ten weekly facilitated sessions that included instruction, professionally made videotaped vignettes, discussion, role-playing, and assignments. The children's program, conducted in the classrooms of participating teachers, involved puppets and other drama therapy techniques to relay related content.

Currently, we are in the final year of our clinical trial. During the previous three years, we conducted INSIGHTS in three schools. At two other schools, we ran an after-school Read Aloud program, which was anticipated to increase the children's excitement about reading but was not expected to change their behavior. The reading program thus served as a control group to our INSIGHTS experimental intervention. A total of 152 children and their parents and 46 teachers participated. Ninety-one parent-child dyads were in the INSIGHTS program, and 61 were in the Read Aloud program.

To evaluate the effectiveness of INSIGHTS, as contrasted with the Read Aloud program, a number of different methods were used. Under the leadership of my collaborator, Dr. Catherine Tamis-LeMonda, parents were videotaped when interacting with their children while they baked microwave cupcakes, completed puzzles, and engaged in clean-up activities. The children and their teachers were observed in their classrooms, and all of the participants answered a number of questionnaires. Parents were also interviewed about their children's behavior throughout the intervention period. Then Dr. Edilma Yearwood conducted extensive postintervention interviews with the participating parents, teachers, and children.

The yield of data from all of these activities is massive. Statistical analyses of the various types of data are under way. Preliminary findings from the first two years of intervention, however, are compelling. INSIGHTS, when compared with the Read Aloud program, significantly reduced child behavior problems, enhanced parenting strategies, and reduced negative teacher strategies. Parents and teachers also reported high levels of satisfaction with the program, a finding that was further supported by what they told us in their own words and by our observations.

The evolution of the INSIGHTS program is ongoing. Our team of researchers and clinicians continues to add components to the program. We look forward to testing the effectiveness of these new techniques in a second clinical trial. Our team is also developing additional ways to disseminate this information to parents and clinicians. Structured workshops, like the ones we are conducting in the elementary schools in New York City, are an example of one approach (McClowry, 1998). Individual and group counseling are other vehicles. This book is yet another way. A careful implementation of the strategies presented here, the same as those we use in the INSIGHTS program, can help parents be more effective in their parental role. The application of the strategies can also be facilitated by clinicians—for example, therapists, advanced practice nurses, and social workers—who work with families in schools or in mental health or social welfare agencies.

Acknowledgments

This book would not have been possible without the assistance of the many individuals who have been part of the INSIGHTS into Children's Temperament project. My extraordinary research collaborators are Catherine Tamis-LeMonda, PhD, a developmental psychologist from New York University's applied psychology department, and David L. Snow, PhD, who is a clinical/community psychologist and director of The Consultation Center at Yale University. Also contributing to the project were Edilma Yearwood, PhD, an RN from Georgetown University, who joined us as a post-doctoral research fellow; Robert Landy, PhD, from New York University's drama therapy department; and Ursula Barr and Charlotte Fritz-Milan, who kept the project going as its coordinators.

I am also grateful to the many graduate students from the departments of nursing, school psychology, teaching and learning, and drama therapy, who enriched our team with their diverse backgrounds. They were the facilitators, coders, data management assistants, and puppet therapists on this complex project. I am delighted that many of these research assistants are incorporating temperament and parenting into their own dissertations and clinical practice: Simone Andrews, Debbie Arnold, Jason Barr, Rahil Briggs, Allyson Carlson, Dana Connolly, Shoshana Dachs, Marie Foley, Pam Galehouse, Jennifer Gullesserian, Jonathan Howie, and Winema Jackson.

Funding for research on the INSIGHTS project was primarily provided by the National Institute for Nursing Research/National Institutes of Health. Preliminary studies were funded by the U.S. Department of Health and Human Services, The Fan Fox and Leslie R. Samuels Foundation, and challenge grants from the Steinhardt School of Education and New York University.

INSIGHTS was conducted in partnership with New York City's Community School District 5. Earlier studies were conducted in New York City's Community School District 13 and several cities in Connecticut: Milford, Orange, New London, Waterbury, and West Haven.

Most of all, I am grateful to the children, parents, and teachers who participated in the program. They were generous with their time, receptive to our proposed strategies, and sincere in their responses. Their commitment to INSIGHTS was matched only by the principals and school district administrators who welcomed us into their schools and communities.

Introduction

Like most parents, it was not until my second child was born that I became a believer in children's temperament. Up until then, I was convinced that my first child, Allison, was a product of the environment that her father and I provided. As an infant, Allison was a cautious observer of the world. She carefully watched the activities going on around her and reacted strongly and negatively to novel situations. My role as her mother was to comfort her. When I did, Allison relaxed and appeared happy, at least until her next encounter with something or someone who was unfamiliar to her.

Allison's negative reactions to novelty continued as she got older. When I took her to the petting zoo when she was two years old, the baby animals frightened her. The only way she would get near them, let alone touch them, was if I gently guided her. It was not until I petted them that she realized it was all right to touch them. Still, her tentative movements came with anxious giggles that signaled that she was near tears and was prepared to cry if the baby animals made any unexpected movements.

At four years of age, Allison cried her way through Disneyland in anticipation that something might be "scary." I remember giving her constant reassurances, trying to convince her that the amusement park was safe and that everything in it was intended for the entertainment of children and their parents. And by the last day of the trip, Allison was relaxed.

My initial belief that the environment, and particularly the parents in it, strongly influences a child's behavior held up for five years, until Allison's brother, Sean, joined our family. He quickly let it be known that he was completely different from his sister, even as a fetus. Whereas Allison's movements while I was pregnant with her were gentle, Sean was vigorous and in nearly constant motion.

Sean was not home from the hospital nursery very long before I recognized other contrasts as well. From the time he was a baby, everyone and everything delighted him. He seemed eager to embrace the world and was easily and enthusiastically amused. As a baby, he spent a week discovering his right foot, giggling every time it moved. The next week, his left foot equally fascinated him.

Sean's eagerness to try new things was even more apparent as he got older. When he went to a petting zoo as a toddler, my job was to protect the baby animals from his vigorous hugs. As Sean got older, he seemed to think that no height was too high to climb.

He also viewed everyone as a potential new friend and lamented that no day was ever long enough.

The striking contrasts between my two children caused me to rethink the role that environment contributes to the individual differences that children demonstrate. Parenting strategies that worked well with Allison were inappropriate for Sean. Allison needed me to soothe her when she encountered new experiences. Sean, on the other hand, needed opportunities to explore the world while I maintained constant vigilance in order to assure his safety.

The distinction between my children remains apparent today, even though Allison is twenty-nine years old and Sean is twenty-four. Allison is a beautiful and gentle woman who is devoted to the critically ill patients she competently cares for as an advanced practice nurse. She and her husband are loyal to their family and committed to their local community. Sean, on the other hand, is a musical composer and performer. He still hasn't found a challenge too difficult to attempt (although now most of his challenges are related to music rather than to scaling heights). Sean is still trying to meet everyone he can and find a way to make his days longer than the 24 hours that most of us consider more than adequate.

Many of the differences between Allison and Sean can be attributed to their temperament. I did not know about child temperament when my children were growing up. I wish I had. I think it would have made me a better parent or at least a more relaxed and confident one. Simply said, temperament is the consistent reaction style that a child demonstrates across a variety of settings and situations, particularly those that involve stress or change. In other words, temperament contributes towards the differences in behavior that children exhibit in reaction to their everyday experiences.

Your child's temperament has a profound impact on his or her development. It also influences your child's perceptions and interpersonal relationships—which is where you come in. As a parent, your responses to your child's temperament are likely to have an impact on his or her behavior and self-esteem. This book is intended to make you more insightful and effective in your responses to your child.

As with any new and broad topic, temperament-based parenting necessitates learning a number of topic-specific (and, as it turns out, quite helpful) terms. As you learn them, the temperament-based concepts on which this book is based are likely to reverberate in other aspects of your life. Suddenly, you will see temperament everywhere. Although the focus of this book is on school-age children, you may find yourself applying the content to your relationships with your spouse or significant other, your siblings, your co-workers, or your own parents.

This book is divided into three parts. Part 1 explains the "three Rs" of parenting: *recognizing* your child's temperament, *reframing* your perceptions of your child, and *responding*, rather than reacting, to your child's temperament. Part 2 focuses on the "two Cs": parental strategies you can use to gain *compliance* from your child and some of the ways that parents and children can communicate how much they *cherish* each other. Part 3 encourages you to apply the content of this book to broader issues. Suggestions on how to foster your child's independence are presented. Developmental concerns that may be currently challenging for your child or that might be in the future are also addressed. Finally, for those who are interested in learning more about temperament, Part 3 also includes additional information on temperament research and, in particular, my own.

As parents, we know the relationships that we have with our children are pivotal to their emotional and social development and to the tenor of our family lives. My sincere hope is that this book will provide you with insights into temperament that will better enable you to relay to your child how much you cherish his or her uniqueness. I also hope that it will guide you in fostering your child's attributes and talents. Such transactions are likely to result in a more pleasurable relationship between you and your child. Nothing between a parent and a child could be more valuable, satisfying, and enjoyable.

PART 1

The Three Rs of Parenting:
Recognize, Reframe, Respond

CHAPTER ONE

Recognizing Your Child's Temperament

Have you ever noticed how children in the same family can be very different? One is friendly and flexible. Another is shy and cautious, and a third, perhaps, is feisty. Temperament is one way to explain the individual characteristics and differences that occur among children, even among those who are members of the same family.

Temperament is defined as the consistent reaction style that a child demonstrates across a variety of settings and situations, particularly those that involve stress or change. The circumstances that prompt a temperamental reaction do not need to be dramatic. One child can interpret an unexpected wait in line for a movie as an opportunity to socialize, whereas that child's sibling may whine relentlessly.

Temperament is also a lens through which individuals view their world. You have probably noticed how some adults tend to have positive reactions to the majority of their daily experiences, yet for others such occurrences are rare. The same holds true for children. Their temperament influences how they perceive and react to the world. In turn, their reactions alter the way others respond to them (Rothbart & Bates, 1998). For example, children who are consistently pleasant and happy are likely to elicit warmth from those who care for them. Because they are usually compliant, such children also make their parents "look good." Other children are grumpy most of the time no matter what the circumstances. Parents and other caregivers are likely to be impatient with a child whose reactions to even minor events are usually contrary. The central premise of this book, which is derived from temperament theory, is that each child is unique and is endowed with attributes and talents that have the inherent potential to blossom in a nurturing environment. When we give birth to a baby or welcome an adopted or foster child into our family, we begin an incredible journey of discovering the essence of that child. Yet children don't come with manuals, and parents end up using a trial-and-error method to learn what strategies satisfy and comfort their specific child. Many books and experts offer generic childrearing advice to parents. Such techniques often fail to be effective, however, because they don't take into account the uniqueness of each child's temperament. Temperament-based parenting, as described here, is in effect a nongeneric approach. It is intended to give you greater insight into your particular child and assist you in developing effective parenting strategies relative to your child's temperament. Once these standards are applied, you will find that your child's daily behavior improves and that family interactions become more relaxed and enjoyable.

Temperament-based parenting is not just about discipline. It also involves learning more about your child's strengths so that you can better appreciate what a special child you have. Children need to know that they are cherished for their uniqueness. Only then can they develop a true sense of security and positive self-esteem. You are probably reading this book because you are already a good parent who wants to be even more effective and nurturing. Implementing temperament-based parenting strategies can contribute towards your goal.

The information in this book is likely to be more relevant if you first take the time to record your perceptions of your child's temperament. I invite you to fill out a questionnaire that I developed, The School-Age Temperament Inventory (SATI; McClowry, 1995a). The SATI (pronounced "say—tee"), as it is known to its friends, has been filled out by thousands of parents in a number of different countries. Parents tell me that filling it out and seeing the results helps them understand how they perceive their child's temperament. There are two ways to complete the SATI. You can create your child's profile by following the directions in the appendix. (If you have more than one child, you may wish to photocopy the inventory first.) If you have access to the Internet, you may find that the easiest way is to answer the questions online at the following website: **www.nyu.edu/education/nursing/insights/**. Select the button labeled "Online Temperament Profile." Follow the directions, and a copy of your child's temperament profile will be immediately generated for you to print out. Once you have your child's temperament profile, put it aside. We will refer to the information on it in the upcoming pages and chapters. But first let me explain the five major principles of temperament.

PRINCIPLES OF TEMPERAMENT

The major principles of temperament are as follows:

1. Children are born with a unique temperament.
2. Temperament influences behavior and emotional reactions.
3. Temperament is easy to see in situations that involve change or stress.
4. Temperament does not change easily.
5. Goodness of fit is the answer.

Principle 1: Children Are Born with a Unique Temperament

Intuitively, most people recognize that whereas individuals are unique, they are also quite predictable. Have you ever heard people say, "It's his nature to be that way"? We all know adults who are consistently cheerful and those who are irritable most of the time. Likewise, we recognize that although some people are generally exuberant, others are reserved.

Temperament involves the intrinsic and stylistic parts of ourselves that contribute towards making us the unique individuals that we are. Our inborn temperament influences the way that we act and react in our lives. Because temperament has a biological basis, babies are born with a particular temperament, although some babies take a few months before they consistently demonstrate it.

As I discussed in the introduction, parents often become believers in temperament when they have a second child. They are frequently amazed at the differences between their children that cannot be attributed to the environment. For example, strategies that worked with a first child may be counterproductive with the second. Whereas the first baby might have giggled when playfully jostled, the sibling might be overstimulated by such an activity and would rather be held quietly and securely.

Principle 2: Temperament Influences Behavior and Emotional Reactions

The second principle of temperament deals with its expression. Observing a child's behavior is one way to assess his or her temperament. Parents have myriad opportunities to be with their children, so they are uniquely suited to describe their children's temperament. That is what you did if you completed the SATI: You based your answers to the questions on your day-to-day recollections of your child. For example, you might already know that your child is always active. Or you may have noticed that your child has difficulty completing tasks like homework or simple household responsibilities.

Of course, all children vary in their behavior to some degree. Even a child whose temperament is generally pleasant will have times when he or she is uncharacteristically grumpy. Anybody, even a little kid, can have a bad day. When we assess a child's temperament, however, we are looking for the child's general predisposition to exhibit a consistent behavioral style.

Temperament is more than behavior—it also involves our internal reactions to situations. Temperament influences how individuals perceive other people and events. It has major implications for how we remember and interpret experiences. You have probably noticed that people often differ in their descriptions of the same situation. Temperament contributes towards their diverse perceptions.

Before we learn more about temperament, it is important to dispel some misconceptions about the concept. Temperament is not a synonym for "temper" or "temper tantrum." Although children with particular types of temperaments are more likely to have temper tantrums or to exhibit their anger, temperament itself is a neutral concept. Consequently, there are not good temperaments or bad temperaments. Temperament, instead, refers to normal variations in individual characteristics. Children with all types of temperaments have strengths and related tendencies that cause parents to be concerned. No type of temperament should be equated with a behavioral disorder or psychiatric diagnosis.

Another misconception is that childhood temperament is the same as adult personality. Most temperament researchers view adult personality as more complex than childhood temperament. Although temperament continues to influence our reactions during adulthood, as we get older we become selective in expressing it. By adulthood, we have had considerable experience interacting with the environment and its constraints. As we internalize the feedback we receive, we often find ways to disguise our temperament. Thus childhood temperament evolves into a more complex adult personality that is also affected by our motivations and abilities. Infants and children, however, are genuinely natural in their expression of temperament. Their reactions to situations are driven by their temperament.

A final myth is that you will become a permissive parent if you take into account your child's temperament. On the contrary, temperament-based parenting doesn't mean that you should accept child behavior that violates your values or is disrespectful. Parents are responsible for socializing their children. In subsequent chapters, you will be presented with a number of effective parenting strategies that match your child's temperament.

Principle 3: Temperament Is Easy to See in Situations That Involve Change or Stress

The third principle explains why temperament is a powerful predictor of children's reactions to change. Every day, multiple situations occur that are likely to elicit reactions from your child that are based on his or her temperament. Change is stressful even when it involves a positive event like going on a vacation.

Disappointments, such as having a sports event rained out, are also stressful. Other circumstances that parents take for granted may also provoke many children to exhibit behavior indicative of their temperament—for example, testing days at school, visits from family members, or holidays. When my children were growing up, my daughter, Allison, anticipated Christmas in her quiet, reserved manner. Her brother, Sean, on the other hand, was even more exuberant than usual for weeks prior to the event.

Children differ on which circumstances they find stressful. Some children find a quiet environment boring and will use everything in their power to increase the level of stimulation, even if their behavior results in negative consequences such as being disciplined. Other children are upset by noise or by events that they easily find overstimulating. These children usually withdraw emotionally in order to make themselves more comfortable.

Principle 4: Temperament Does Not Change Easily

The fourth principle advises us that attempting to change a child's temperament is futile. Because temperament is inborn and partly hereditary, it is highly resistant to change. The environment, and particularly the parents in it, can put constraints on a child's behavior, but no one can change the child's intrinsic makeup. Efforts to change a child's temperament are frustrating for both the parent and the child and are likely to be counterproductive. Such strategies undermine the child's self-esteem because they relay the message that you are not pleased with the child. This book will not teach you methods to change your child's temperament. Instead, the focus is on enhancing "goodness of fit," as explained in the next and final principle.

Principle 5: Goodness of Fit Is the Answer

Stella Chess and Alexander Thomas (1984), pioneers in the temperament field, first explained the fifth principle of temperament. They maintained that a child's adjustment is enhanced through "goodness of fit." Goodness of fit is the match of the child's temperament to the demands, expectations, and opportunities of the child's environment. When goodness of fit occurs, positive development can be anticipated. On the other hand, when there is a mismatch or "poorness of fit" between the child's temperament and the environment, behavior problems are likely to develop.

As an adult, you have probably been in situations or had jobs that afforded you goodness of fit. How did you feel? You were probably comfortable in that environment and felt appreciated for your contributions. Think about how different that experience was from other times, when you encountered poorness of fit. Now, imagine being seven years old and experiencing poorness of fit with your first-grade teacher. Young children cannot quit school or move to a new school district. They are also limited in their ability to identify and discuss their distress. Instead, they may become sad and withdraw or act out their frustration.

Effective parents adjust the environment in their home to achieve goodness of fit for their children. Goodness of fit, however, must be evaluated within the context of the family environment. Depending on their own temperament, philosophy of childrearing, and expectations for their children, parents may find that children with particular types of temperament are easier than others to handle. Some children are just easy to parent. They are naturally pleasant and compliant. If a child has an easy temperament, parents may erroneously attribute the child's good behavior to their superior parenting. Instead, they may have just been fortunate to have a child with an easy temperament. These children also tend to thrive even under less-than-ideal circumstances. Researchers regard such children as resilient.

Other children have more challenging temperaments that can provoke even the most caring of parents. Children with challenging temperaments often make simple interactions with their parents complicated and stressful. Negative patterns of interaction between parents and the challenging child often become repetitive. Although temperament may be innate, our society still blames parents, and particularly mothers, if a child exhibits negative behavior. In time, parents of such children are likely to feel that others are criticizing their parenting skills. Likewise, parents of such children often assume that the child is intentionally acting in a frustrating way. Maybe not. It could be that the child is just reacting in a way that is consistent with his or her temperament. As my son, Sean, once said to me after I scolded him for being, in my opinion, overly exuberant, "You tell me to be myself. But when I am, I get in trouble."

Providing goodness of fit within the context of a family is further complicated when the temperaments of siblings are widely different. My son, Sean, thrived on cultural events and other stimulating city experiences. His sister, Allison, preferred the security of a small suburban community. Consequently, we lived in the suburbs and spent a great deal of time driving Sean to the city so he could engage in cultural events.

Enhancing goodness of fit entails implementing the three Rs of temperament-based parenting: recognize, reframe, and respond. The first step is to *recognize* your child's temperament. You have already begun that process by observing your child and completing the SATI. An additional way to recognize your child's temperament is to compare and contrast the information in this book with your own experiences of your child. For example, as you learn about the four dimensions of temperament, described next, think about your child. Does he or she demonstrate a tendency to be high or low on these dimensions? In chapter 2, we'll compare your overall impressions of your child's temperament with the information you provided on the SATI.

DIMENSIONS OF TEMPERAMENT

Child temperament includes four dimensions:

1. Activity
2. Approach/withdrawal
3. Task persistence
4. Negative reactivity

Activity

Activity refers to motor activity. It is the child's tendency to move around and to be active. Children who are high in activity are constantly in motion, even when they are supposed to sit still. Children who are low in activity can sit quietly for long periods of time and may even need encouragement to engage in sports and other motor activities.

Approach/Withdrawal

Approach/withdrawal is evident in the child's first reaction to new people or new situations. Children who are high in approach are usually excited about meeting new people or having an opportunity to experience a novel situation. Often they will initiate such experiences. Children who are low in approach (and thus high in withdrawal) appear to be shy. They withdraw from new people or new situations. If, however, children who are high in withdrawal are given time to adjust, they usually become more positive in their reactions.

Task Persistence

Task persistence is the child's tendency to stick with a task until it's done, even if he or she is interrupted. Children who are high in task persistence can complete their schoolwork or other activities with ease. They also seem to derive satisfaction from such accomplishments. Children who are low in task persistence have difficulty finishing homework or other projects without a concerted effort.

Negative Reactivity

Negative reactivity is the child's tendency to have negative reactions to life situations. A child who is high in negative reactivity will have an intense, immediate negative reaction to a minor inconvenience. The child may exhibit high negative reactivity through facial expressions, body language, tone of voice, or statements of distress or displeasure. Some people talk about such children as having an "attitude." In contrast, the child who is low in negative reactivity is generally pleasant and mild in his or her reactions to situational changes.

✳✳✳

This chapter ends with an exercise to help you apply what you have learned so far. Over the next few days, observe how your child deals with a change in activities or with a stressful experience. Select a minor event, record what happened, and assess whether you recognize any dimensions of temperament. For example, what reaction did you see when you insisted that the television be turned off at bedtime? Another situation might be prompted by a change in plans, such as postponing a visit to a friend's home. Or what happens if your child plans to wear an outfit but finds out that it is not clean and he or she must wear something else?

As you complete the exercise, concentrate on *how* your child reacts (which is his or her temperament) rather than on *what* your child does (which is his or her behavior). For example, if you ask your child to finish her homework assignment and she does not, does she exhibit her usual tendency to be low in task persistence by looking around the room or starting other activities? Or if you ask your child to put away his toys because it is bedtime, does he grumble in a way that is consistent with his tendency to be high in negative reactivity?

The next chapter includes additional examples that can help you recognize your child's temperament. You will also learn the next step in the three Rs of parenting: how to reframe your perceptions.

Parent Observation Guide

1. What was the mildly stressful situation?

   _____

   _____

   _____

   _____

2. How did your child react?

   _____

   _____

   _____

   _____

3. What dimension of temperament (activity, approach/withdrawal, task persistence, or negative reactivity) do you think he or she exhibited?

   _____

   _____

   _____

   _____

CHAPTER TWO

Reframing Your Perceptions of Your Child's Temperament

If you have taken the opportunity to observe your child and complete Parenting Exercise 1, you are probably becoming more aware of how temperament influences your child's behavior and reactions. This chapter goes into more detail about the ways to recognize your child's temperament, describing how to create a temperament profile for your child and introducing you to the Dynamic Four—characters who illustrate four common temperament profiles. At the end of the chapter, you will be encouraged to apply what you have learned to reframe your perceptions of your child's temperament.

As suggested in chapter 1, there are primarily two ways to recognize your child's temperament: Through your intuitive impressions about your child or by feedback you receive in the form of your responses on the SATI. Either approach or a combination of both is appropriate because temperament-based parenting starts with your perceptions of your child. Your relationship with your child and your responses to his or her behavior are also highly related to your perceptions.

If you use intuitive impressions to recognize your child's temperament, you are estimating how your child matches each of the dimensions. If you rely on this method, you will pay close attention to those parts of this book that resonate with you because they seem to describe your child. The feedback approach, on the other hand, results in a *temperament profile* developed on the basis of your answers to the questions on the SATI.

THE TEMPERAMENT PROFILE

Children can be high, medium, or low on each of the four temperament dimensions described in chapter 1: activity, approach/withdrawal, task persistence, and negative reactivity. When we talk about a child's temperament, we are actually referring to those dimensions on which the child is high or low.

Let's use Jodi's Temperament Profile, shown in Figure 1, as an example. Jodi's parents completed the SATI, in the appendix of this book, and computed an average score for each temperament dimension according to the instructions given there. They then

FIGURE 1
Temperament Profile for Jodi

NEGATIVE REACTIVITY	TASK PERSISTENCE	APPROACH/ WITHDRAWAL	ACTIVITY
HIGH	HIGH	WITHDRAWAL	HIGH
⬤ **X**	△	◯	⬤ **X**
		X	
△	◯ **X**	△	△
LOW	LOW	APPROACH	LOW

compared Jodi's average scores to fixed values (given in the appendix) and marked the appropriate boxes for each dimension.

When applying temperament-based strategies, the dimensions on which a child scores either high or low are considered *salient*. These are the boxes with triangles and circles on the profile form. When Jodi's parents compared her scores on the SATI with pretermined values, they found that her salient temperament dimensions are high negative reactivity, low task persistence, and high activity. Her parents marked these boxes with an *X*. Jodi's scores fell in the plain center box on approach/withdrawal (neither high nor low), so her parents marked that box. In applying temperament-based parenting principles, Jodi's parents will focus primarily on her salient temperament dimensions.

Parents often report that children whose salient temperament dimensions are in the boxes with circles exhibit more *challenging* behaviors than those whose scores fall in the boxes with triangles. Conversely, children whose salient temperament dimensions are in the boxes with triangles are usually regarded as *easy* by their parents. This generality, however, needs to be qualified with a reminder that no temperament is ideal in every situation, as we will discuss later in this chapter. Likewise, because parents differ in the attributes that they value or find frustrating, the easy and challenging descriptors may not apply in all instances.

If a child scores in the middle row (the plain boxes) on any of the dimensions, it is likely that he or she may not react consistently on that dimension. For example, a child whose task persistence score falls in the middle-row box may be persistent in some situations—for example, when playing a musical instrument. The same child may lack task persistence at other times, such as when being told to complete his or her homework. The inconsistency on that dimension means that it is not a salient part of the child's temperament, but is likely to differ based on his or her motivation or circumstances.

Temperament-based parenting is applicable to most children. In my study of 883 children, 98.5 percent were high or low on at least one of the four temperament dimensions (McClowry, 2002a). Consequently, almost all children have at least one salient temperament dimension on which to apply temperament-based parenting.

Occasionally a child will, based on feedback from the SATI method, score in the middle of all four dimensions. Does that mean that the child does not have a temperament? Of course not. It might mean that the child has an unusually mild temperament. Another possibility is that the parents' description of the child is particularly gentle. In such cases, parents can use the intuitive impressions approach. Another reason to use intuitive impressions is if feedback on the SATI produces a profile that does not match parents' overall impressions of the child's temperament. If this is true in your case, you can still apply the parenting strategies that, based on your intuitive impressions, seem to match your child.

THE DYNAMIC FOUR

Some parents find that a *temperament typology* is more helpful to them in recognizing their child's temperament than one based on scores for each of the dimensions. In the study of 883 children mentioned previously, 42 percent of the children had temperaments that matched on one of four common temperament profiles, which I call the Dynamic Four (McClowry, 2002a).

Over the years, I have introduced the Dynamic Four to a variety of audiences: young children, parenting groups, professionals, and other temperament researchers. In my observations, I have noticed that many children and adults tend to gravitate towards the profile that is most like them. Sometimes they react negatively to one of the other profiles, as if they were in conflict with that type of person. My clinical impression is that many people recognize themselves as one of the Dynamic Four. Adults and children also often comment that one or more of the profiles remind them of people in their lives.

In the children's version of the INSIGHTS program, the Dynamic Four are represented by puppets who resemble the characters shown in this book (McClowry, 2002b). At the end of the program, we ask the child participants to tell us whether they think that they are similar to any of the puppets and, if so, to explain why. We also ask them to select the puppet that they would most like to have as their best friend. The comments of the first and second graders demonstrate how insightful young children can be about their own temperament and that of their friends. After each of the descriptions of the profiles, I have added some of the comments made by these children. (For the purpose of illustration, the profiles show only the characters' salient dimensions.)

Let me introduce you, then, to the Dynamic Four. They are Freddy the Friendly, who is social and eager to try; Coretta the Cautious, who is cautious and slow to warm up; Hilary the Hard Worker, who is industrious; and Gregory the Grumpy, whose temperament is high maintenance. See if any of them remind you of your child.

As you get to know the Dynamic Four, remember that there are two ways to describe a child's temperament. One way is to discuss the child's salient temperament dimensions, as we just did. Another way is to talk about the temperament typologies—the Dynamic Four. You may find that, based on your intuitive impressions or on feedback from the SATI, one or two of the Dynamic Four may have characteristics that match your own child's. Some children, however, will not match the types because they have a temperament that is high or low on a different combination of dimensions. In such cases, focus on the salient temperament dimensions that do match your child's temperament. Also keep in mind that, although the Dynamic Four have names indicating that they are male or female, they could be represented by either gender. The profiles could just as easily have been named Felicia the Friendly, Carl the Cautious, Harold the Hard Worker, and Georgiana the Grumpy.

Freddy the Friendly

- **Low in negative reactivity**
- **High in approach**

NEGATIVE REACTIVITY	TASK PERSISTENCE	APPROACH/ WITHDRAWAL	ACTIVITY
HIGH	HIGH	WITHDRAWAL	HIGH
◯	△	◯	◯
△ X	◯	△ X	△
LOW	LOW	APPROACH	LOW

Freddy the Friendly's temperament profile shows that he is social and eager to try. He is driven by his need to be with people and to try new experiences. He is high in approach and low in negative reactivity. Consequently, Freddy is usually pleasant and has a zest for life that often draws others to him. Friends and family are important to Freddy. He greets new experiences with enthusiasm because they provide additional opportunities to meet and be with people.

Freddy is usually excited about going to school because it gives him a chance to be with his friends. Freddy's mom, however, worries about his safety. She thinks that he may get into trouble because he is so eager to try new experiences and make new friends. She is also concerned because, in his eagerness to try new things, he may not always demonstrate the best judgment regarding his safety.

In my research, 9 percent of the children were described by their mothers as having a profile like Freddy the Friendly's (McClowry, 2002a). When we asked the first and second graders in the INSIGHTS program to select the puppet most like them, children who perceived themselves to be like Freddy made the following comments:

> "I'm really happy sometimes, and sometimes I'm just a little too friendly."

> "I am friendly, and it is easy for me to meet new people. I can go to people and tell them my name."

The children who chose Freddy as their best friend did for these reasons:

> "Because he's friendly and nice to people."

> "Because he likes to share his stuff."

Coretta the Cautious

- **High in negative reactivity**
- **High in withdrawal**

NEGATIVE REACTIVITY	TASK PERSISTENCE	APPROACH/ WITHDRAWAL	ACTIVITY
HIGH	HIGH	WITHDRAWAL	HIGH
X	△	X	○
△	○	△	△
LOW	LOW	APPROACH	LOW

Coretta the Cautious has a temperament profile that suggests she is slow to warm up. Because she is high in withdrawal (and thus low in approach), her first reaction is to withdraw from new situations and new people. Coretta is also high in negative reactivity, often letting you know that she is not pleased by changes or stressful situations. Some people think that Coretta is shy. With time and an appropriate amount of support, however, Coretta usually feels more comfortable and is then able to respond more pleasantly.

In my research, 8 percent of the children were described by their mothers as having a temperament profile like that of Coretta the Cautious (McClowry, 2002a). The children in the INSIGHTS program who perceived themselves as being most like Coretta made the following observations:

"Every time I go in a new class, I get shy."

"When my mommy gets mad, I cover my face and get cautious."

The children in the program were often protective of Coretta, as evidenced by some of the comments of those who wanted her to be their best friend:

"Because I want her to be more friendly."

"I can help her a lot and she can lighten up."

Hilary the Hard Worker

- **Low in negative reactivity**
- **High in task persistence**
- **Low in activity**

NEGATIVE REACTIVITY	TASK PERSISTENCE	APPROACH/ WITHDRAWAL	ACTIVITY
HIGH	HIGH	WITHDRAWAL	HIGH
○	△ X	○	○
△ X	○	△	△ X
LOW	LOW	APPROACH	LOW

Hilary the Hard Worker has a temperament profile that shows her to be industrious. Because she is high in task persistence and low in activity, she can sit for long periods of time doing schoolwork or a puzzle, or while playing with her toys. She likes to get things done and takes pleasure in her accomplishments.

When there is a change in plans, Hilary usually handles the disappointment well because she is low in negative reactivity. However, Hilary has been known to object when she is not permitted to finish an activity she has started or when she does not feel that she has completed it to her level of satisfaction. Hilary is a good student who likes to please her teacher. Her parents, however, think that Hilary needs help learning to be more assertive about getting her own needs met.

In my research, 6 percent of the children were described by their mothers as having a temperament profile like that of Hilary the Hard Worker (McClowry, 2002a). The children in the INSIGHTS program who viewed themselves as most like Hilary made the following statements:

"I'm a hard worker. I can do my work without running around."

"I do all my work, sit down, and listen to the teacher. I can finish my work easily."

Those children who chose Hilary as their best friend did so for the following reasons:

"Because she's a hard worker. If she was in my class and I didn't know how to do my work, she could help me."

"Because we like to do the same things. I'd let her be first, and I'd be second."

Gregory the Grumpy

- **High in negative reactivity**
- **Low in task persistence**
- **High in activity**

NEGATIVE REACTIVITY	TASK PERSISTENCE	APPROACH/ WITHDRAWAL	ACTIVITY
HIGH	HIGH	WITHDRAWAL	HIGH
X	△	○	X
	X		
△		△	△
LOW	LOW	APPROACH	LOW

Gregory the Grumpy's temperament profile shows him to be high maintenance. He reacts strongly and negatively to change or stress because his temperament is high in negative reactivity. Gregory gets upset easily and can be very moody. Some people have said that he has an "attitude." His dad prefers to think of Gregory as just being honest.

Gregory often has problems completing tasks such as putting away his toys or finishing his homework assignments because he is low in task persistence. Gregory is also high in activity. Consequently, he has difficulty sitting still. He wiggles constantly.

On the positive side, Gregory's high activity level often energizes his classmates and siblings. Sometimes he ends up in a leadership position. Gregory can be an effective leader because he is comfortable making decisions and expressing his opinions, even when others disagree.

In my research, 8 percent of the children were described by their mothers as having a temperament profile like that of Gregory the Grumpy (McClowry, 2002a). The children in the INSIGHTS program who viewed themselves as being like Gregory gave the following explanations:

"I walk around the class a lot, and I don't do my homework."

"If my mother tells me something and it doesn't go my way, I get grumpy."

Of the four temperament profiles, the children in the program chose Gregory least often to be their best friend. Even though we try to make the puppet version of Gregory a sensitive sort of grumpy person, the children frequently describe him as "mean." Still, a few of the children expressed empathy for Gregory, as the following quote implies:

"Sometimes he's friendly and he needs a friend."

One startling observation is that children even as young as first grade can identify themselves as having a high-maintenance profile. A small number of the children selected Gregory as a best friend because they recognized their own reactions as being similar to his:

"Sometimes I can be grumpy like him."

When these findings are transferred to real life, they help us to understand that children whose temperament is like Gregory's often have interactions with others that are uncomfortable or frustrating. If you have a child whose temperament profile is like Gregory's, recognize that being high maintenance is not easy. The Gregories of this world perceive minor situations as difficult to handle and are easily distressed by them. Likewise, many people find dealing with Gregories to be challenging. Temperament-based parenting principles, however, can help parents deal more effectively with such children by avoiding excessive responses to their negative reactivity. Likewise, by using temperament-based principles, parents can teach such children to express themselves in ways that are less distressing to those around them.

The Dynamic Four provide striking evidence that children differ in their temperament in substantial ways. In addition to the children who are described by one of the four profiles, some children have very easy temperaments (McClowry, 2002a). About 4 percent of children in my research were both industrious like Hilary the Hard Worker and social/eager to try like Freddy the Friendly. Another 6 percent of children had temperaments that were very challenging; they were high maintenance like Gregory the Grumpy and cautious/slow to warm up like Coretta the Cautious.

Now that you've met the Dynamic Four, let's look at Jodi's temperament profile again, on page 18. Notice that, based on the feedback method, Jodi's temperament matches Gregory the Grumpy's (in other words, her combination of dimensions is the same as his).

A FEW CAUTIONS ABOUT LABELING

An important distinction needs to be made between recognizing a child's temperament and labeling him or her with it. The temperament profiles are intended as reference points with which parents can compare and contrast their child's behaviors. Parents can gain insights into their child's temperament by exploring whether any of the profiles are similar to their perceptions of their child's temperament. Even if a child does not match any of the profiles, examining them helps to clarify how the child differs from children who do.

Caution, however, must be exercised in telling someone, including your child, that you perceive him or her to be like one of the profiles. As demonstrated by the children's comments in the INSIGHTS program, many young children can identify their own temperaments. Self-identification, however, is different from being labeled by someone else. Telling a child that he or she is similar to one of the profiles may give the impression that you do not recognize the child's uniqueness. Particularly if the profile has characteristics that you may not value, your child may feel misunderstood. For example, saying, "You are just like Gregory the Grumpy" is likely to be hurtful to the child, especially if it is said in anger.

Instead, insights into your child's temperament should be respectful and spoken about judiciously. Adult caregivers may want to exchange information about their perceptions of a child without engaging him or her in the discussion. If a child initiates a conversation that includes self-identification of temperament, it is best to listen attentively and sensitively. You may wish to follow up with benign and supportive questions, such as "What kind of things are easy for Coretta to do? Are those easy for you also?" or "What kind of things are challenging for Coretta? Are those challenging for you also? What would help you to meet those challenges?"

No temperament is ideal in every instance. As the next section describes, every temperament has strengths. In addition, each temperament has related issues that are likely to cause parents concern.

REFRAMING YOUR PERCEPTIONS

At this point, you have considered a number of ways to recognize your child's temperament. Once you recognize your child's temperament, you can advance to the next step, which is to reframe your perceptions. Reframing is a powerful temperament-based parenting strategy that enhances goodness of fit. It allows parents to appreciate their child's strengths while simultaneously acknowledging child temperament–related problems or concerns. No temperament is ideal in every situation. Depending on the child's temperament, the child may find that some things come naturally and are easily managed. Other situations are challenging because they require the child to stretch beyond his or her innate tendencies. A skillful parent can anticipate what type of situations are challenging for the child and will provide the necessary support.

Based on what you know about your child's temperament, check off in the first column of Table 1 the salient temperament dimensions that apply to your child. Then note what strengths accompany those dimensions in the second column. Related problems and parental concerns that match your child's temperament dimensions are listed in the third column. A temperament-based exercise to help you apply the content of this chapter to your child is included on page 28. In chapter 3, you will learn how to match your parental responses to your child's salient temperament dimensions to enhance your parental effectiveness.

TABLE 1
Dimensions of Temperament: Strengths and Possible Concerns

Dimensions	Strengths	Possible Concerns
High task persistence	Usually completes assignments or jobs without a lot of reminders.	May have difficulty stopping an activity once he or she begins something. May also try to do everything perfectly.
Low task persistence	Can easily switch from one activity to another. May be very creative.	Needs supervision to complete homework or other tasks.
High approach (low withdrawal)	Social and willing to try new things and meet new people.	May be willing to take too many risks. Parents are likely to have safety concerns regarding the child's tendency to talk to strangers and try new experiences.
Low approach (high withdrawal)	Careful. Does not rush into situations.	Shy or unwilling to try new activities or meet new people.
High activity	Energetic.	Has difficulty sitting still.
Low activity	Quiet.	May not engage in enough physical activities or sports.
High negative reactivity	Honest.	Complains frequently.
Low negative reactivity	Easy to get along with.	May go along with the group without considering the consequences. May need to be more assertive.

Reframing

Observe your child. Describe a minor event. Include in your description what you have learned in this chapter about your child's salient temperament dimensions. Be sure to use the information from Table 1 as your guide.

1. What was the situation?

   _____

   _____

   _____

2. What salient temperament dimension(s) did your child demonstrate?

   _____

   _____

   _____

3. What strengths can you see in relation to the dimension(s) of your child's temperament?

   _____

   _____

   _____

4. What problems or concerns may be related to the dimension(s) of your child's temperament?

   _____

   _____

   _____

CHAPTER THREE
Parental Responses

Chapters 1 and 2 have focused on the manifestations of your child's temperament and your recognition of it. Building on what has already been presented, this chapter emphasizes the ways that your parental responses influence your child's development and affect family interactions.

Every day, a plethora of situations occur that require parents to respond to a child's behavior or requests. Many of these are, from an adult viewpoint, minor events. From the perspective of a child, however, the situations can seem monumental. As discussed previously, vacations, holidays, tests at school, and cancelled events can prompt a temperamental reaction. The case is the same with mundane situations, such as forgetting to bring a completed homework assignment to school or misplacing something.

The type of situation to which a particular child reacts and the manifestations of that reaction are related to the child's temperament: Hilary the Hard Worker might be excited about conducting a class science project, whereas Gregory the Grumpy might find such an assignment annoying. As the science project evolves, however, other reactions could occur. Hilary might become upset if she could not devote enough resources or time to it or if she feels that her finished product does not live up to her expectations. Gregory, on the other hand, might complain that the task is taking too long and that it is interfering with other activities in which he would rather be engaged.

As the following diagram illustrates, a child will usually react to one of these "life happens" situations in a way that is consistent with his or her temperament. A parent, in turn, can respond to the child's reaction in a variety of ways. Some parental responses are more effective than others. In this chapter, we will talk about three categories of parental responses: *counterproductive, adequate,* and *optimal.* Several examples of each will be presented.

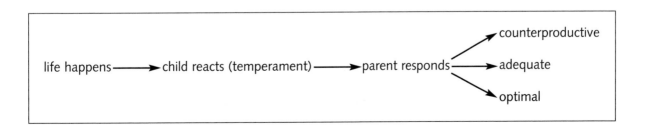

Counterproductive: A parental response that only makes the situation worse. Usually, counterproductive responses are delivered in an angry tone of voice.

Adequate: A parental response that is intended to get the situation resolved quickly and is spoken in a neutral fashion.

Optimal: A parental response that is intended to help the child mature. It acknowledges the individuality of the child by remarking about his or her temperament or desires. Optimal statements are relayed in a warm, understanding manner.

Notice that the way the response is delivered is an integral component of the message the parent gives the child. Statements that acknowledge the individuality of the child but that are delivered without warmth relay a mixed message. Likewise, harsh statements that are made with a smile generate an equally confusing message. Mixed messages are hurtful to children because children typically internalize only the negative part of the communication.

COUNTERPRODUCTIVE PARENTAL RESPONSES

To illustrate the three categories of parental responses, we will examine how a minor event has the potential to escalate into a negative spiral of reactivity between a parent and child. Getting ready for school in the morning can be a stressful time for families and can elicit a number of temperamental reactions and, in turn, parental responses. Consider what might happen if Coretta the Cautious, who is high in negative reactivity, was unable to find her purple barrettes while she and her mom are rushing to get her to school on time. Missing barrettes constitutes a "life happens" situation in a way that will test Coretta and her mother. At 7:47 A.M., this could cause a dilemma.

Coretta: Mom! Mom! I can't find my purple barrettes.

Mom: Do you remember when you last wore them?

Coretta: If I remembered, would I be asking you?

Mom: That's no way to talk to me, young lady. If you would put your things where they belong, you would be able to find them, and we wouldn't have to deal with your problems. I don't know why you do this!

Coretta: You don't have to yell at me for nothing!

Mom: For nothing? You need to put your barrettes away where they belong! If you did, you wouldn't be running into this problem. And I will not have you speak to me that way.

In response to her daughter's temperamental reaction, "If I remembered, would I be asking you?" Coretta's mom replied with a *counterproductive* statement. She lectured Coretta about putting her things away. As illustrated in the scenario, her counterproductive response just made the situation worse. Such responses are especially ineffective with children like Coretta, who are high in negative reactivity, because they trigger a negative spiral that does nothing to resolve the problem. If we were to observe Coretta and her mother as they continued to interact, it is likely that Coretta would raise her voice even louder with each subsequent statement, as would her mother. By the time their verbal battle was complete, Coretta and her mother would be guaranteed to be frustrated with each other, and the barrettes would most likely remain missing. Table 2 describes several types of counterproductive responses.

In the course of everyday life, all parents periodically use counterproductive responses. If my children were asked about the parenting responses I used when they were growing up, they would report many instances in which I nagged or lectured them. Being able to identify when we use counterproductive responses is a critical first step to reducing the occurrence of these interactions and replacing them with others that are more effective.

One of the reasons counterproductive responses should be avoided is that they allow the child to be more powerful than the parent. They fuel destructive transactions between the parent and child that can escalate into defiant noncompliance by the child. Counterproductive responses can also bring about a situation in which the parent demonstrates a loss of control by verbally or physically hurting the child. In contrast, adequate and optimal statements put the parent back in charge of the situation.

ADEQUATE PARENTAL RESPONSES

Adequate parental responses are recommended for most situations. The intent of such responses is to resolve a situation quickly and effectively. They are "adequate" because they simply ask that life progress with mutual respect and courtesy. When using such responses, the parent relays the expectation that the child will be compliant so that the situation can be resolved. Table 3 lists several types of adequate responses.

If Coretta's mother had used an adequate response when her daughter was upset about the missing barrettes, it is likely that the scenario would have progressed in a different fashion. For example, Coretta's mom might have taken command by matter-of-factly responding in the following way.

Coretta: Mom! Mom! I can't find my purple barrettes.

Mom: They're in the wicker basket under your bed.

Using an adequate response was a good choice for Coretta's mom because her daughter's temperament is high in negativity. Moreover, given the time pressures involved in getting off to school and work, a straightforward answer can be effective in quickly resolving an issue.

TABLE 2
Counterproductive Parental Responses

Nagging	Repeating the same message over and over.
Lecturing	A scolding that goes on and on and often involves a discussion of previous mistakes the child has made.
Withdrawal	A passive and ineffective response that is indifferent to the child and/or that does not help the child to solve his or her dilemma. (Withdrawal is different from "ignoring," which is done intentionally and effectively, as will be discussed later.)
Hassled	An irritated response, spoken while the parent is paying attention to something else.
Teasing	Talking to the child in a way that taunts or teases the child or is sarcastic.
Nattering	A nonverbal expression of parental displeasure used when a parent does not deal with the child's behavior directly. Instead, the parent makes a face, uses a gesture—like shrugging his or her shoulders—or says something sarcastic about the child. A nattering response can also be a negative comment about the child directed to someone else while the child is listening.

Two types of adequate responses require further explanation. Parents are encouraged to adopt and consistently use a *signal*—a device that is effective as a first-step disciplinary strategy. A signal can be a single word said with a particular inflection, such as quietly saying the child's name. Or it can be a specific facial expression or motion, such as raising one eyebrow or using a benign hand gesture. Signals are a powerful private communication between a parent and child. They give the child a warning that his or her behavior is becoming unacceptable. No one else needs to witness the interaction. If you use a nonverbal signal, be sure that you have your child's attention before you deliver it. Whether the signal is nonverbal or verbal, maintain eye contact with the child until he or she acknowledges receiving the signal.

If you are going to use a signal, use the same one consistently so that your child will immediately recognize it. There is another critical guideline for using signals: They should be used only once in a particular situation. If the signal does not work the first time, an effective parent will advance to another strategy, like the ones that will be discussed in chapter 6. Using a signal more than once diminishes its power for future use because it allows the child to think that it does not require his or her immediate compliance. In addition, it allows the child to take over the interaction rather than keeping the parent in control.

Table 3
Adequate Parental Responses

Taking command Giving the child a directive in clear, simple language.

Using humor A light, jovial, and caring response. When humor is used sincerely, it can lighten a situation and prompt a resolution.

Cooling down Being calm when the child is overexcited or angry. This response is particularly effective when the response is given in a slow, quiet voice.

Signaling Giving the child a quiet verbal or nonverbal warning.

Ignoring An intentional effort to ignore the child's behavior. (Ignoring is especially useful for remarks made by children who are high in negative reactivity.)

Ignoring is another powerful, adequate parental response and one that has been examined extensively by researchers (Baden & Howe, 1992; Patterson, 1982). One point regarding ignoring cannot be stressed enough: Effective parents exercise a great deal of discretion in determining when to engage in transactions with their children and when to ignore a situation or comment. Ineffective parents, on the other hand, overreact to trivial situations that are best ignored. Rather than neutralizing a child-initiated negative interaction, ineffective parents escalate it, as we have already discussed, by making counterproductive responses, such as reacting in an irritated manner.

Determining when to ignore and when to get involved is complicated. In general, if there is a concern about the child's safety, a parent must get involved. In other circumstances, particularly those in which the child seeks attention but that are not destructive, ignoring can be an appropriate strategy. For example, a child might be whining because her favorite television show is not on that evening. An effective parent will briefly acknowledge the child's disappointment, then ignore further expressions of distress, even if the child increases the volume of the complaints. However, in some circumstances, as will be extensively discussed in chapter 5, attention seeking on the part of the child might be quite legitimate and best handled by spending time together in a way that satisfies the child's need for parental attention.

Under no circumstances, however, does ignoring allow a parent to abdicate his or her parental responsibility. Instead, the parent should continue to discreetly monitor what is going on with the child, but not react or respond unless the child's behavior becomes unsafe. For example, minor sibling squabbles should be ignored when the children are old enough to resolve their own disagreements. A statement such as "I know that you two kids can decide which television program to watch without my help" is another appropriate adequate response. Still, the vigilant parent should remain attentive to what is going on between the siblings to assure that one is not taking advantage of the other and a balanced resolution occurs.

Ignoring is an indispensable parenting strategy when a child's temperament is high in negative reactivity. Because it is impossible to remake a child who is high in negative reactivity into a sunny individual, a parent needs to be judicious in selecting times to negotiate and times to ignore. If a parent responds to every negative comment such a child makes by attempting to soothe or make the child happy, a power switch occurs. A well-intentioned parent who appreciates the importance of negotiating may inadvertently encourage the child who is high in negativity to become a family tyrant. Such children can quickly learn that, by expressing distress, they can control the parent and dominate the family dynamics.

Some parents find ignoring particularly difficult to do. Parents whose own temperament is high in negative reactivity often readily engage in negative spirals of reactivity with their children of like temperament because they, themselves, are reacting rather than responding. The remedy in such situations is for parents to become consciously aware of their reaction style and then to decisively implement more effective parenting strategies, like the adequate ones just discussed, as well as optimal ones.

OPTIMAL PARENTAL RESPONSES

The third category of parental responses is called *optimal.* These responses are intended to foster a child's development, not just to gain his or her compliance. By definition, optimal responses relay parental warmth while still conveying expectations for mature behavior.

One type of optimal response encourages the child to problem-solve a "life happens" event. In contrast to an adequate parental response, in which a parent uses a directive to resolve the situation, an optimal response engages the child in exploring possible solutions. Encouraging the child to problem-solve supports his or her sense of competence and independence.

A second kind of optimal response acknowledges that you have heard the child's wishes but that circumstances or expectations for behavior require you to deny his or her request. For example, your child may want to go to a vacation location that is not financially feasible for your family. An optimal response would be, for example, "I really wish that we could afford to go to Alaska this summer, but we can't. Instead, I hope we all have fun visiting at Grandma's house during our vacation." The first part of the statement, "I really wish" tells the child that you have heard him or her. The "but" portion of the interchange reasserts parental control and guidance.

A third type of optimal response tells your child that, although you recognize his or her temperament, the situation dictates that he or she will have to respond in a way that transcends it, even though the child may be somewhat uncomfortable doing so. Such a statement is not in any way intended to change the child's temperament; rather, it offers support while the child navigates a course of action that is challenging. Table 4 lists optimal statements related to child temperament. Notice that these examples use the "but" convention to relay parental expectations for behavior in a supportive way. Using what you have already learned about your child's temperament, determine the ones that apply to your child.

If you have not previously used optimal responses, I encourage you to try them. You may find that, at first, optimal statements may startle your child because they deeply communicate that you recognize and appreciate his or her individuality. But the surprise, I promise you, will be a pleasant one for your child.

Part of the success achieved from implementing optimal responses and other strategies from temperament-based parenting is learning which strategy to use when and how often. As with other powerful techniques, optimal statements should be used with discretion. The overuse of optimal statements decreases their effectiveness. When employed constantly, children become bored with them and do not react at all.

Likewise, optimal statements are best reserved for moments when there is adequate time for the parent and child to engage in an interaction that fosters the child's development. For example, Coretta's mom might have responded with an optimal statement if there had been enough time to resolve the case of the missing barrettes. The scenario could have proceeded in the following manner.

Coretta: Mom! Mom! I can't find my purple barrettes.

Mom: If I remember correctly, you and Susan were playing with them when she was here. Do you remember where you left them?

Of course, there is no guarantee that using an optimal parental response will result in a positive resolution. Even if Coretta's mom used an optimal statement that was intended to encourage her daughter to resolve her own problem, Coretta might have reacted negatively. Although optimal statements do not always produce successful interactions, counterproductive responses, most assuredly, lead to calamitous consequences.

A FAMILIAR SCENARIO: "HE HIT ME"

Before we leave this chapter, we will observe another scenario that occurs with children of every temperament. As all parents know, fighting between siblings or friends can happen at any moment. Children who are high in negative reactivity are particularly likely

---

TABLE 4

Optimal Parental Responses

Low task persistence	"I know that you would prefer not to work on your homework right now, but . . ."
High task persistence	"I know that you would prefer to continue to play right now, but . . ."
High approach	"I know that you love to try new things, but do you think it would be safe to . . ."
High withdrawal	"I know this is new for you, but . . ."
	"I know that sometimes you would rather watch than join the other children, but . . ."
	"I know that it is sometimes hard for you to make a change, but . . ."
High activity	"I know that you like to run and jump and that you are really good at it, but . . ."
Low activity	"I know that you prefer quiet activities, but . . ."
High negative reactivity	"I know that you are just being honest, but it's important to me that . . ."
Low negative reactivity	"I know that you try hard to get along with your friends, but . . ."

---

to engage in such encounters. In this scenario, Gregory and Freddy are playing with their cars when an outbreak of "He hit me" occurs. Freddy's mom sees the minor altercation, noting that neither boy is hurt. Freddy's mom handles the "life happens" situation in a number of different ways. As you read them, try to identify whether her responses are counterproductive, adequate, or optimal.

Freddy: Mom! Gregory hit me.

Mom: All right, Gregory and Freddy. Each of you needs to collect your own cars and play separately for five minutes. I'll set the timer.

Freddy's mom takes control by using an adequate response. She resolves the issue in a matter-of-fact way that presents the boys with a negative consequence for their inability to get along.

Freddy: Mom! Gregory hit me.

Mom: Maybe Gregory didn't mean it. Sometimes kids bump into each other by accident. Did he say he was sorry, or did he try to get out of your way?

Freddy's mom uses an adequate response to cool down the situation. Her comments are intended to help Freddy reinterpret the event in a more benign way and prevent the situation from escalating.

Freddy: Mom! Gregory hit me.

Mom: Gregory, why did you do that to Freddy? When are you going to learn how to play together without fighting? You two are always fighting.

This counterproductive response includes lecturing. Notice that Freddy's mom does not take any decisive action to correct the situation.

Freddy: Mom! Gregory hit me.

Mom: Sometimes when children are playing with cars, it's easy to get in each other's way. Maybe you guys need to give each other more room. How could you give each other more space?

This parental response is optimal because Freddy's mom tries to assist the boys in resolving the problem themselves.

Freddy: Mom! Gregory hit me.

Mom: I saw what happened. You pushed him, and then he hit you. You are just trying to get him in trouble. You always think that everyone is picking on you, but it's you that always starts the fights. Why can't you kids get along?

Freddy's mom uses another counterproductive response by nagging Freddy. He, in turn, is likely to try to defend himself, which is unlikely to be effective because the interaction with his mom began so negatively.

Freddy: Mom! Gregory hit me.

Mom: *(Sighs and shrugs.)*

Freddy's mom demonstrates a nattering counterproductive response. She neither acknowledges Freddy nor acts decisively to resolve the situation.

Freddy: Mom! Gregory hit me.

Mom: Gregory and Freddy, come here. All right, boys, what are the rules of our home regarding playing together?

The parental response is optimal: Freddy's mom engages the boys in resolving the issue by having them remind each other of the house rules.

Freddy: Mom! Gregory hit me.

Mom: "Mom! Gregory hit me. Mom! I'm a baby. I can't handle my own problems."

This response is blatantly counterproductive. Freddy's mom is ineffectively responding to the situation by teasing and taunting Freddy. Freddy is likely to feel misunderstood. He is also likely to conclude that he cannot expect his mother to assist him in difficult situations.

Freddy: Mom! Gregory hit me.

Mom: *(Looks away and gives no response.)*

This passive, withdrawn response by Freddy's mother is counterproductive. Freddy is likely to escalate his complaints until he gets her attention.

Freddy: Mom! Gregory hit me.

Mom: Freddy and Gregory! We do not allow hitting in our home. If one of you hits the other again, I will take Gregory home immediately.

Freddy's mom demonstrates an adequate parental response. She clearly states her expectations for behavior and the consequence that will follow if they are violated.

Freddy: Mom! Gregory hit me.

Mom: Freddy, can't you see I'm busy?

The hassled response that Freddy's mom makes is counterproductive. She does not address the fighting issue at all.

Freddy: Mom! Gregory hit me.

Mom: And how are you and Gregory going to resolve this issue?

Engaging in a discussion of "who hit whom" and "why" is likely to make the situation worse. Instead, Freddy's mother uses an optimal response by attempting to get the boys to resolve their own problems.

Now that you have had an opportunity to observe the responses of Freddy's mother, it is time to focus on your own. Consider implementing a signal as an adequate first-step response in a disciplinary strategy. The following exercise is intended to help you identify which type of parental responses you use. In chapter 4, we will discuss how to contract with your child to gain compliance over repetitive annoying behaviors.

Observing Your Own Parental Responses

1. Every parent uses a counterproductive response now and then. Can you remember one that you have used? Please describe it.

_____

_____

2. How did your child react to your counterproductive response?

_____

_____

3. Describe an adequate response that you have used.

_____

_____

4. How did your child react?

_____

_____

5. Use an optimal statement in response to your child. Explain what it was.

_____

_____

6. How did your child react?

_____

_____

PART 2

The Two Cs: Gaining Compliance and Cherishing Each Other

Chapter Four
Gaining Compliance

Mark Twain once said, "My mother had a great deal of trouble with me, but I think she enjoyed it." At least according to her son, Twain's mother appears to have been more bemused by him than annoyed. Not every parent, however, has such a reaction. Some parents report that they often feel frustrated with their child, particularly when he or she is noncompliant.

In chapter 3, we examined how parental responses to children can be optimal, adequate, or counterproductive. We also discussed the impact of counterproductive responses on a child's subsequent behavior. In this chapter, we will explore how counterproductive responses can become so incessant that they undermine parental authority and damage the parent-child relationship. The temperament-based framework previously discussed will be expanded to assist you in appraising the overall quality of your parent-child interactions. The use of a parent-child contract will be suggested as a strategy to improve your child's behavior and enhance your dyadic relationship—that is, the dynamics unique to the two of you. The content will be further expanded to describe how you can advocate for your child in settings outside your home, such as at school or in community organizations. Collaboration with your child's teacher will be highlighted.

PARENT-CHILD RELATIONSHIPS

By their very nature, parent-child relationships have enormous potential for intimacy. The unique connection between a parent and his or her child elicits interactions that are emotionally rich with meaning. Positive relationships can bring great joy to both parties. Conversely, conflict between a parent and child can be very painful. Most parents and children are resilient enough to weather occasional frustrating incidents. Still, as with all relationships, it is important to frequently review the tenor and quality of the ongoing interactions. The following pages describe how a caring parent-child relationship can evolve into one that is troublesome. Recognizing such patterns at an early stage can help parents alter this course before their interactions become coercive and resistant to change.

Repeated incidents of conflict between a parent and child have the potential to accumulate until they escalate into deleterious interactions, a series of transactions that adversely affect the relationship, the child's development, and parental satisfaction. One example of such a transactional pattern, a spiral of negative reactivity, was described in chapter 3. By definition, spirals of negative reactivity take place when a child has a temperament that is high in negative reactivity. Children with other types of temperament, however, can also have troublesome transactions with their parents. Although individuals who are high in negative reactivity can especially provoke intense and disagreeable interactions, all dyadic relationships have the potential to evolve into conflictual patterns.

Conflict between a child and parent begins when one of the two fails to live up to the other's expectations. A number of factors can contribute to this predicament. A parent might have expectations that are unrealistic because they are inconsistent with the child's temperament, developmental age, or aptitude. Another reason might be that the child's temperament is so high in negative reactivity, or in withdrawal, that he or she would frustrate almost any caregiver.

A conflictual pattern may also be initiated when a parent responds counterproductively to a child who is acting benignly. Of course, all parents have days when they are overtired and overstressed, but some parents consistently respond harshly to simple requests their children make. The child's temperament is likely to influence how he or she reacts to a parent's irritated response. A child who is high in negative reactivity is prone to initiate a negative spiral of activity. The parent's irritated response is likely to be met with an equally harsh remark by the child that will fuel the fire and add further momentum (and volume) to the discussion.

Children who are low or average in negative reactivity may respond in a more complicated manner but still arrive at the same outcome. They may either try to appease their parent or attempt to avoid additional interactions. Neither of these reactions is psychologically healthy because, by engaging in them, a child circumvents his or her own needs in order to avoid upsetting the parent. If this pattern continues, the child will assume the parental role, and the dyadic communication will become progressively more distorted. Eventually, the parent, the child, or both will become frustrated and angered by the distorted communication.

Over time, interactions like the ones just described are likely to result in a grim deadlock that can be described as "getting stuck." Minor annoyances between a parent and a child occur repeatedly until they escalate into high levels of conflict and misunderstanding. The struggle eventually becomes so emotionally charged and embedded with negative expectations that it is easily evoked and often repeated. A parent-child dyad engaged in this degree of struggle eventually respond to each other in habitual, nonreflective ways (Mezirow, 1990).

Getting stuck has serious repercussions for a family. The parent feels powerless when attempting to gain child compliance. The situation is further fueled if the parent is counterproductive in his or her subsequent response. The impact on the child is equally dramatic. Although it may not be obvious to the parent, a child who is frequently successful in winning a power struggle with his or her parent experiences a significant loss. Children expect their parents to be more powerful than they are so that they can feel protected. If parents are not in control, children lose confidence in their parents' ability to help them behave in a manner that they know is consistent with the family's values and also socially acceptable. Strategies from temperament-based parenting can be applied to "unstick" the interactions between parent and child and to change them into more productive and satisfying ones. The parent can change his or her perspective of the child by reframing, as discussed in chapter 2. Another way is to implement a parent-child behavior contract as a strategy to change the child's behavior.

BEHAVIOR CONTRACTS

Behavior contracts are recommended for repetitive, frustrating behavior problems. If your child is regularly engaging in some activity or behaving in some way that annoys you and that you have not been able to resolve, then it is likely that implementing a contract will be advantageous. Some parents initiate contracts after they recognize that they are stuck in a painful battle of wills with their child. Others wisely apply the strategy at an earlier stage of frustration.

The purposes of behavior contracts are threefold. First, a repetitive, annoying child behavior is extinguished or at least greatly reduced. Equally important is the second purpose, which is to switch the power base. A successful contract shrinks the child to a more age-appropriate size at the same time the parent regains his or her authority. In the process, a third objective is achieved: A recurring negative interchange between the parent and child is replaced with a more positive one.

While conducting the INSIGHTS program, we noticed that the behaviors that were the focus of parent-child contracts were remarkably commonplace. Ordinary events had become extremely disruptive within the family's life. Parents told us that they struggled with their school-age children on organizational issues like putting away their toys or backpacks, selecting what clothes to wear for school, making their beds, bringing homework assignments from school, completing the work, and/or returning it to school the next day. Process-oriented issues included the manner in which children talked to their parents, transitioning between events, fighting with siblings, and respecting the rights of other family members by honoring agreed-upon quiet times or locations.

Child temperament is often related to these situations. Children who are low in task persistence tend not to be organized. Those who are active may have difficulty settling down or being quiet. Children who are high in negative reactivity may express themselves in ways that upset others.

Parental expectations, which may be a reflection of the parents' own temperament or the way they structure their lives, may also play a part. For example, parents who need quiet time after they return home from work may find it difficult to respond to a child who desires a lot of interaction in the evenings. Parents who are organized may be less tolerant of children who are not. I had frequent squabbles about organizational matters with my son, Sean. Although he attended the same schools as his sister, he claimed that the school never asked him to bring home any notes or announcements. The only exception was notices about violin lessons, which somehow managed to make it home. Looking back over our struggles, I wish that I had engaged Sean in a contract that focused on his organization. More than likely, it would have helped. In other words, let me suggest you use a strategy that I regret I developed only after my children were already grown but that parents in the INSIGHTS program have found very successful.

GUIDELINES FOR CONTRACTING WITH YOUR CHILD

A behavior contract is a carefully negotiated agreement between you and your child. The guidelines for establishing a contract are summarized in Table 5. At first glance, these steps may appear simple. Further exploration will convince you that they require a concerted effort on your part. The satisfaction gained by resolving the situation, however, will compensate you for the time and effort involved.

Before you initiate a contract with your child, you need to take some preliminary steps. First, identify one specific behavior that your child frequently exhibits that annoys you. Then analyze the components of the situation carefully so that you can select one reasonable goal on which to construct the contract. Remember that you want the child to be successful in achieving the goal, so be sure that it is not just feasible, but easy to achieve. For example, if your conflict with your daughter is related to her messy room, choose one aspect on which to concentrate first. The contract might deal with putting away her toys before bedtime or depositing her dirty clothes in the hamper or making her bed—not with cleaning her entire room. Or if your son has difficulty moving from one activity to the next—that is, transitioning between events—focus on a component of getting ready for school, such as eating breakfast or getting in and out of the bathroom in a timely manner. The reason for selecting one simple goal is to guarantee the success of the contract.

Once you have decided upon a goal, think about how you can word it in a positive way. The phrasing is especially important if the

---

TABLE 5

Guidelines for Contracting with Your Child

1. Select one reasonable goal.

2. State the goal in a positive way.

3. Negotiate child and parent (and teacher, if appropriate) responsibilities.

4. Decide together on a reinforcement. (It can be a privilege or a small item.)

5. You and your child (and teacher) should sign the contract.

6. Check the goal at the specified time. If achieved, place a sticker on a tally sheet; otherwise, leave the space blank.

7. Give no warnings.

8. Acknowledge your child when he or she meets the goal. Use optimal statements whenever possible.

9. Be sure to provide the child with the reinforcement when the contract is completed.

---

behavior has become embedded in a negative transactional pattern between the two of you. Some goals require a great deal of creativity to state positively. For example, if the goal is to get your child to stop whining, you could describe it as "talking in a grown-up voice" or "speaking in a pleasant voice when asking for help."

After you have done your initial planning, begin the formal negotiation process with your child. I recommend that you invite your son or daughter to join you in a quiet spot in your home, such as the kitchen table or your desk. Set a tone to the meeting to convey that you are taking the contract seriously. Be prepared by having something to write with, a copy of the contract (see Parenting Exercise 4, on page 54), and a copy of the Behavior Contract Tally Sheet (see page 56). Explain to your child that you have been reading a book about becoming a better parent. One of the homework assignments in this book (children love it when their parents have homework!) is to develop a contract to change a situation that has been a problem for the family.

Begin the negotiation process with your child by suggesting that you start the contract with the goal that you suggest. Tell your child that the goal can be changed in a week or two and that he or she can select the next one. Most children enjoy the contracting process and are willing to begin with the parent's idea, especially when they realize that they will have input on other components. If, however, your child is opposed to the goal you selected, you will need to find one that is agreeable to both of you. It makes no sense to design a contract intended to enhance compliance if your child is in opposition to it from the start.

Once the goal is agreed upon, discuss your respective responsibilities. For example, if the goal is to keep the living room in a more presentable condition by picking up toys before bedtime, the child's responsibility might be to place the toys in the closet by 8:30 P.M. It follows that your responsibility will be to check whether the goal has been accomplished at 8:30 P.M.

If the selected goal is more process oriented, find a way to limit it to a particular time, at least for the first week. For example, if the goal is to talk in a grown-up voice, make it specific by adding "during dinner" or "while getting ready for school." You can extend the amount of time or change the conditions in subsequent weeks.

The next item of negotiation has two parts. Determine the number of times that your child must achieve the goal before he or she receives a reinforcement. Again, it is important to be reasonable so that your child can be successful. The contract should not require your child to be perfect. If homework assignments are given five days a week, negotiate for four days of compliance. Or if your child is supposed to make his or her bed before eating breakfast, set the initial goal for five days out of the possible seven.

The selected reinforcement should be something minor like a privilege or a small item. Reinforcements selected by the parents and children in the INSIGHTS program were trading cards, a play date, a movie, or a special dessert or other food item. Remember that the reinforcement is a tangible way of telling your child that you acknowledge his or her effort to fulfill the responsibilities on which you agreed. Anything more elaborate than a small object or gesture will become the focus and weaken the effect of the contract.

To emphasize the importance of the contract, you and your child should sign it, as shown in Figure 2. As the final step before implementing the contract, have your child assist you in placing the dates on the tally sheet. Then display the tally sheet and the contract in a place of prominence, such as on the refrigerator door.

Once the contract is in place, follow it carefully, even on days when it is inconvenient. For example, if you promise to check your child's room to see whether the bed is made in the morning, be sure to do so. On days when your child is successful in fulfilling the agreed-upon responsibility, verbally acknowledge him or her as you place a sticker on the tally sheet in the designated space. (If you do not have stickers, you can draw something like a smiley face or a star.) Use optimal statements whenever possible.

On days when your child does not fulfill his or her responsibilities, do not reprimand the child. Leave the tally space blank and say something matter-of-fact, like "You can try again tomorrow." Such a statement, when said in a neutral tone, informs the child that you are taking the contract seriously but is unlikely to trigger the old battle between the two of you. Refraining from making anything more than a neutral statement can be difficult for some parents, especially those who frequently engage in counterproductive responses such as nagging or lecturing.

FIGURE 2
Sample Child-Parent Behavior Contract

Child's name _Allison McClowry_

Parent's name _Sandee McClowry_

Goal _Select clothes for school before you go to bed._

Child's responsibilities _Allison will select her clothes for school before she goes to bed from Sunday through Thursday._

Parent's responsibilities _Mom will check Allison's room before she goes to bed to see whether Allison has picked out her clothes. Allison will get a sticker in the morning if she did._

Reinforcement _A friend can spend the night on Saturday if Allison gets at least four stickers that week._

Sandee McClowry

Parent's signature

Allison

Child's signature

Another way that well-intentioned parents can undermine the contract is by giving the child a reminder or a warning if the responsibility is not completed. A single reminder or warning is appropriate in other situations, as will be discussed in chapter 6. Reminders or warnings, however, should not be used when a contract is in place because the identified responsibilities have already been negotiated.

The same principles apply to the reinforcement that you and your child have agreed he or she will receive at the conclusion of the week if the agreement is satisfied. Acknowledge the child if he or she has earned the reinforcement. If your child is unsuccessful in achieving the reinforcement, evaluate whether the goal was too ambitious for an initial one. Amend the contract for another week by selecting a more realistic goal. If your child receives the reinforcement, amend the contract for the second week to expand the responsibilities slightly. For example, you might add a task related to cleaning up the child's bedroom, such as putting all dirty clothes in the hamper before bedtime.

Be sure to keep the contract active with weekly amendments for three to five weeks. When your child is consistently fulfilling the contract, end it by holding another meeting with your child. Acknowledge the progress made on both of your parts in improving the child's behavior and in communicating with each other. Suggest to the child that the contract no longer seems necessary. Be sure, however, to recognize and praise your child when he or she continues to fulfill the goals on which the contract was based. If you terminate the contract too quickly or do not continue to recognize your child verbally, you may find that he or she slips back into the annoying behavior that preceded the contract (or that you begin using counterproductive responses again). Before things deteriorate to their previous level, implement a new contract or reinstate the old one.

Some behavioral problems are best handled by including more than one adult in the contract. The second adult may be your child's other parent or someone else who is engaged in caring for your child. For example, problems related to homework may be more effectively managed if the child's teacher is also a contracting partner. The next section of this chapter offers suggestions on engaging another caregiver in the contracting process.

ADVOCATING FOR YOUR CHILD

The ideal way to raise a child is to have consistency among caregivers regarding their expectations for child behavior and use of disciplinary strategies. Such agreement among adults is not easily achieved, but it is more likely to occur if the caregivers share the same childrearing philosophy and strategies. In general, parents and other caregivers, including teachers, deal with children in the same manner that they were dealt with in their own childhoods unless they have had a transformative learning experience (Mezirow, 1990). Temperament-based parenting can provide such an experience, resulting in relationship enhancement and use of more effective child management strategies.

As positive as this outcome is, it often comes with one complication. Once an adult has adopted temperament-based parenting, it is easy to become frustrated with those who have not. Suddenly, the counterproductive responses of other caretakers become readily apparent. Unless careful steps are taken, the tension that existed between a parent and child prior to implementing temperament-based parenting can be replaced by frustration between or among caretakers.

Changing dynamics between two members of a family or within a group is likely to reverberate among others within the group constellation (Minuchin, 1974). The effect can be positive if it results in enhanced communication among the adults involved. Such alliances can also broaden the success of temperament-based parenting. In the introduction, I encouraged you to share what you learn from this book with others who are also caregivers of your child.

The same principles apply to settings outside the home, particularly to your child's school. Children spend a great deal of time with their teachers, who are likely to encounter some of the same annoying behaviors parents do. Do not assume that your child's teacher is aware of the importance of child temperament. He or she may share your frustration but may be unaware of the temperament-based strategies that you are learning. Most teachers have not been exposed to temperament theory in their teacher preparation programs, although many of them intuitively appreciate each child's uniqueness. Others could enhance their relationships with their students and improve their students' academic achievement if they understood how temperament influences behavioral and academic outcomes.

With a better understanding of your child's temperament, you may need to be your child's advocate. Once they understand what you are trying to achieve, teachers can be excellent partners with parents in implementing a contract that focuses on school-related child behavior problems. Goals that would best be handled collaboratively by a parent and a teacher are those that require home and school involvement—for example, homework completion.

The Child-Parent Behavior Contract can easily be adapted to include two adult caregivers by adding another name on the sheet. To gain the cooperation of your child's teacher, you will need to explain how the contract works and why you are implementing it. You and the teacher will need to collaborate on all of the steps already described and agree about the responsibilities of everyone concerned. An example of a completed Child-Parent-Teacher

Behavior Contract appears in Figure 3, and a blank contract to complete is included as Parenting Exercise 5. If you decide to put this type of contract in place, you can use the same tally sheet as for the Child-Parent Behavior Contract.

Figure 3

Sample Child-Parent-Teacher Behavior Contract

Child's name _Sean McClowry_

Parent's name _Sandee McClowry_

Teacher's name _Mrs. Barron_

Goal _Sean will write his homework assignment in his notebook._

_____

Child's responsibilities _Sean will copy his assignment from the chalkboard to his notebook._

Parent's responsibilities _After dinner, Mom will give Sean a sticker if he has written down his assignment._

Teacher's responsibilities _Mrs. Barron will place her initials by the assignment when Sean shows it to her._

Reinforcement _Sean gets a pack of baseball cards on Saturday if he has at least four sets of Mrs. Barron's initials and at least four stickers from Mom._

Sandee McClowry   _Sean McClowry_

Parent's signature   **Child's signature**

Mrs. Barron

Teacher's signature

Child-Parent Behavior Contract

Child's name _____

Parent's name _____

Goal _____

_____

Child's responsibilities _____

_____

_____

Parent's responsibilities _____

_____

_____

Reinforcement _____

_____

_____

_____   _____
Parent's signature   Child's signature

Your Child's Unique Temperament: Insights and Strategies for Responsive Parenting
© 2003 by Sandee Graham McClowry. Champaign, IL: Research Press. (800) 519–2707.

Child-Parent-Teacher Behavior Contract

Child's name _____

Parent's name _____

Teacher's name _____

Goal _____

_____

Child's responsibilities _____

_____

Parent's responsibilities _____

_____

Teacher's responsibilities _____

_____

Reinforcement _____

_____

_____   _____

Parent's signature   **Child's signature**

_____

Teacher's signature

Behavior Contract Tally Sheet

Goal _____

	Monday	Tuesday	Wednesday	Thursday	Friday	Saturday	Sunday
Dates							
WEEK 1							
Dates							
WEEK 2							
Dates							
WEEK 3							
Dates							
WEEK 4							

Your Child's Unique Temperament: Insights and Strategies for Responsive Parenting © 2003 by Sandee Graham McClowry. Champaign, IL: Research Press. (800) 519–2707.

CHAPTER FIVE
Expressing Warmth

Consistently, the child development literature notes that parenting consists of two factors: discipline and warmth (Baumrind, 1966; Kochanska, 1990). Several of the chapters in this book emphasize temperament-based discipline strategies. An equally important but more elusive topic is the focus of this chapter: the expression of warmth.

The vast majority of parents love their children and would do nothing intentionally to harm them. Yet many parents are unaware of how important the expression of warmth is in positively influencing their children's immediate and lifelong psychological development (Lamb, Hwang, Ketterlinus, & Fracasso, 1999; Maslow, 1968). Feeling loved is a universally shared desire and an important precursor to enjoying life fully and loving others.

Parents have varying levels of comfort and skill in conveying their love to their children. Unfortunately, expressing warmth does not come naturally to some parents, and so they refrain from doing so. Other parents compromise their efforts to be warm by simultaneously attempting to discipline their children. Even parents who are usually comfortable relaying positive feelings and observations to their children may have difficulties in certain circumstances and could benefit from enhancing their skills. In this chapter, temperament-based strategies for expressing warmth are described; these include engendering trust, communicating affection, paying attention, and affirming goodness and talents. Ways to encourage a child to be assertive are also explained from a temperament-based framework.

ENGENDERING TRUST

A newborn is completely dependent on his or her caregivers for food, shelter, comfort, and attention. If the mother and other significant caregivers are sensitive and consistent in meeting the needs of the baby, the infant develops the overall impression that the world is, in general, a trustworthy place. Babies who experience such responsive and loving care are indeed fortunate. Psychological development has its genesis in the early caregiving relationships, particularly the one between the mother and her baby. Yet a sense of trust is not an achievement that develops only in infancy. Instead, it is a process that is dynamically challenged and revisited throughout the lifespan (Erikson, 1985).

The sense of trust initiated during infancy between a baby and his or her primary caregivers has the potential to mature during middle childhood. Although children dramatically expand the scope of their world during the school-age years, their parents remain vital nurturers who help them navigate their experiences. Engendering trust with a child during the school-age years requires that parents and children alike expand their horizons. As they get older, children increasingly engage in social contexts beyond their immediate families. Parents can enable their children to adjust to challenges outside the home by socializing them to regulate their behavior appropriately. When this regulation occurs, the parent engenders a deeper sense of trust from the child. Simultaneously, the child gains trust in himself or herself by exhibiting behavior that is suitable for the situational demands.

Engendering trust in school-age children is enhanced through temperament-based parenting. Engagement in settings outside the home is likely to elicit expressions of temperament because such experiences can, at least initially, be stressful. For example, children who are low in approach (and thus high in withdrawal), like Coretta the Cautious, may be reluctant to meet new children. Those who are high in approach, like Freddy the Friendly, might get overly exuberant. Children like Hilary the Hard Worker, who is high in task persistence, may be concerned that their performance may not be adequate. Those who are high in negative reactivity, like Gregory the Grumpy, might resist any alterations in their plans.

The effective parent acknowledges the child's temperamental tendencies while assisting the child to adapt to challenging situations. Although sensitive parents seek out comfortable settings for their children, it is not always possible to find settings that are a perfect match for children's temperament. Nor from a developmental perspective is it judicious to keep school-age children from settings that legitimately stretch their repertoire of skills and behaviors. Coretta the Cautious might decline to participate in experiences that initially make her feel uncomfortable. Yet her parents know that she is likely to enjoy such opportunities if she is given a little support. Imagine the following scenario, and notice how often Coretta's mom, Ms. Lewis, not only shows sensitivity to Coretta's temperament, but also uses effective strategies to support her.

Ms. Lewis: Coretta, I got a call from Amy's mom while you were at school. Amy has invited you to her birthday party on Saturday.

Coretta: I don't want to go. I won't know anyone there.

Ms. Lewis: Actually, you will. Melissa will be there, and so will Heather. I checked with Heather's mom, and she said we could pick Heather up on the way to the party. What do you think?

Coretta: Well, maybe.

Ms. Lewis: Whether you go or not, we should get Amy a birthday present. What kind of things does she like?

Coretta: She likes dolls.

Ms. Lewis: What could we get her?

Coretta: Maybe an outfit for one of her dolls.

Ms. Lewis: That's a good idea, Coretta. What do you think about going to the store after lunch?

Coretta: Well, okay.

Ms. Lewis: Speaking of outfits, if you go to the party, what would you like to wear? How about your blue dress or your new jeans outfit?

Coretta: I don't want to wear a dress. I want to wear my jeans.

Ms. Lewis: Then I'll make sure that your jeans are clean for the party. It sounds like you are getting more interested in going to the party, Coretta. Have you decided you want to go?

Coretta: Are you sure that Heather is going to be there?

Ms. Lewis: Not only is she going to the party, but we are going to pick her up on the way. How about helping me to set the table so that after lunch we can get to the store to buy Amy's doll a new outfit?

Ms. Lewis used several effective strategies to support Coretta. She gave her some control in the situation by not mandating that Coretta attend the party. Instead, she allowed Coretta to have some time to adjust to the idea so that she could anticipate it in a more positive way. Ms. Lewis also engaged her daughter in some of the decisions surrounding the party, such as the type of present to purchase for Amy. She also encouraged her to select her own outfit. Most important to Coretta, she told her that some of her other friends would be at the party and arranged to have one of them accompany her.

Ms. Lewis obviously knows her daughter well and is aware of the level of support that she needs. If Coretta were particularly shy or very young, she might have offered to stay at the party, at least for a while. Instead, she realized that a friend was likely to provide an adequate amount of support to make Coretta feel comfortable going to the party.

Because of Ms. Lewis's sensitive and developmentally appropriate way of handling the situation, Coretta will probably enjoy the party without feeling overwhelmingly anxious. With continued support from her parents, Coretta is likely to feel less, but still some, distress when new situations occur. As she gets older, she will probably gain insight into her own temperament so that she can acknowledge her discomfort when encountering new circumstances. She will have learned an essential lesson: If she is willing to endure temporary uneasiness, it will pass after a short amount of time and may lead to more positive experiences for her. Moreover, if Ms. Lewis continues to be as supportive as she is in the scenario, Coretta will know that she can rely on her mother when she is feeling unduly uncomfortable. Supporting a child through a temperamentally challenging situation engenders trust. It also is a way of expressing warmth. Communicating affection is another way.

COMMUNICATING AFFECTION

Affection communicates a desire to be connected with another and can be expressed in a multitude of ways. Beginning in infancy, children learn to interpret and express emotions through touch and other related physical manifestations, such as facial expressions and body postures. Family traditions and other cultural mores convey to children acceptable norms for touching (Montagu, 1995). Adults and families, as a unit, vary in the manner and circumstances in which they express affection. Some are physically demonstrative and enjoy hugging, kissing, and cuddling, whereas others are more restrained.

Individual differences also play a part in the expression of affection. Within families, each child has his or her own propensity for being touched and for touching in return. Even as infants, children differ in their responses to being touched. Some are cuddly and seem to mold into their parent's arms when they are held. Other babies stiffen when they are picked up. Still, being touched is vital for the emotional health of children. It increases their sense of security and reduces their anxiety (Schanberg, 1995).

Although people should not accept or relay physical affection that they find distasteful, the expression of affection is not a fixed attribute but one that can be taught as a strategy to enhance interpersonal relationships (Montagu, 1995). Learning to be physically demonstrative can require a concerted effort for some individuals, at least at first. One of the parents in our program described her attempts to be more affectionate with her children. She told them that she had learned in her INSIGHTS program classes that she was supposed to hug them. "So" she said in a booming voice, "come here, so I can hug you." Her children jokingly responded in mock horror to her request. But she proceeded to give them quick hugs despite their tongue-in-cheek rebuke. Regardless of the awkwardness of the interaction, it was clear from her description that she managed to communicate her affection in at least two ways. Not only did her children receive hugs, she also managed to let them know that she was working hard at being a good parent and that she was willing to incorporate new strategies even if they were a stretch for her.

As school-age children become more independent and spend greater amounts of time with their peers in group activities, the way that parents convey their affection becomes less overt. For example, rushing out to home base to hug a 10-year-old after he has scored a home run will meet with a great deal of understandable resistance from the child and his coach. Instead, affection between parents and their school-age children is often communicated in nonphysical ways. Eye contact, accompanied by a smile in response to something your child did, can relay that you are connecting with him or her, even if no words are issued. Verbal comments describing how you enjoy or appreciate his or her attributes are also ways of being affectionate. Simply telling your child directly that you love him or her during an appropriately private moment is also expressing warmth very effectively.

When a parent attempts to communicate affection, all of the verbal and nonverbal components should relay a positive sentiment to avoid sending the child a mixed message. The affirmative content of the verbal message should be accompanied by a caring tone of voice. The message is most clear when parent and child are directly facing each other and when there is eye contact and a gentle touch. Yet, on a practical basis, elegant moments of intimacy are infrequent. Because of this, parents are advised to take advantage of the naturally occurring situations that allow for quick expressions of affection, such as when transitioning from the soccer field to the car or while setting the kitchen table.

Communicating affection is seriously compromised when it is coupled with critical statements. Notice the differences in these three statements, made by Freddy's dad.

Statement 1: Freddy, you really were a good friend to Coretta today on the playground. She looked sad until you asked her to play with you.

Statement 2: Freddy, I know that you have enjoyed playing with your friends this afternoon, but it's time for us to leave because Mom will be coming home from work soon and we promised to pick her up at the train station.

Statement 3: Freddy, I know that you're friendly, but it gets you into all kinds of difficulties because you pick friends who are really troublemakers.

It is easy to imagine Freddy's dad delivering Statement 1 with a gentle voice and a hand placed on his son's shoulder. Statement 2 is an adequate parental response: Freddy's dad recognizes his son's temperament but appropriately asserts his parental authority in stating that it is time to leave. Although he can deliver the statement affectionately if he uses an empathic tone of voice, the real intent of the message is to acknowledge Freddy's dilemma (play with friends or leave Mom stranded at the train station) in order to gain his compliance. As an adequate parental response, its overall message is neutral. Statement 3, however, is truly a mixed message. Although it begins in a manner similar to that of Statement 2, the second part of the message is critical of Freddy and his friends. After hearing that statement, Freddy is unlikely to know whether his dad values his friendliness or not. Because being friendly is an intrinsic part of his temperament, Freddy is likely to feel confused and hurt.

Affection can also be communicated in tangible ways. I remember visiting my family after I had moved away from home but when my younger siblings were still living there. I noticed that the pantry in our home included a large assortment of cereals. When I asked my mother why so many types were necessary, she rattled off each family member's name with his or her respective cereal of choice. My mother communicated affection in this instance by keeping a supply of everyone's favorite food choice. These subtle displays of affection can, over time, be the very essence of warm childhood memories. Attentiveness is yet another way to express warmth.

PAYING ATTENTION

Paying attention to a child requires empathy and the dedication of time. One facet of empathy is being sensitive to the subtleties that make an individual unique. Children need to know that their parents have identified and cherish their individuality. As already discussed in chapter 3, recognizing a child's temperament and using optimal statements communicate to the child that you are sensitive to his or her uniqueness. Another way is to be aware of and support your child's particular interests, whether in dance, sports, or a particular academic subject. Investing your own time by participating in these interests is another way of paying attention. For example, you might take your child to the museum to see a dinosaur exhibit if that is her interest or applaud your child's efforts at a swim meet if that is his.

Time is a limited commodity, and well-intentioned parents can be so busy meeting the tangible needs of the family that their emotional energy may be depleted when it comes to being attentive to their children. How can caring parents meet the legitimate needs of their children for attention when they have multiple, competing familial and professional demands? The first step is to discern what those needs are from the perspective of temperament.

Temperament often influences the type of attention that children desire and the manner in which they seek it. Children who are high in approach, like Freddy the Friendly, enjoy interacting and are likely to initiate conversations with their parents or try to draw them into shared activities. When involved in new situations, those who are low in approach and who have a tendency to withdraw, like Coretta the Cautious, may wish a parent to be their comfort zone. Children who take great pride in their accomplishments and who are high in task persistence, like Hilary the Hard Worker, may wish for parental recognition of their achievements. Others who are high in negative reactivity, like Gregory the Grumpy, may have complicated ways of getting attention. Their need to express their distress may override their desire for parental approval. In other words, even if their complaints meet with parental sanctions, they may continue to demonstrate their negative reactivity as an attention-seeking ploy.

Although children with temperaments high in negativity may be particularly prone to seek attention through complaining, most children will resort to an assortment of methods to get their parents' attention if they are not receiving what they consider to be an adequate amount. A complicating factor for parents is that children appear to have their own individually determined quota system regarding their needs for attention. Unfortunately, children are not usually explicit in telling their parents how much is necessary. Instead, most will resort to inappropriate ways of getting their parents to notice them if their quota is not fulfilled. Verbal reprimands or even physical punishment may be endured if the need for parental attention is not adequately satisfied.

The fact that children vary in the amount of attention they need should not surprise parents. After all, they differ in the amount of food they require to be adequately nourished. They also vary in the time it takes them to acquire math concepts or to attain athletic skills. Yet some parents worry that they will spoil their children if they spend too much time with them. In our commodity-oriented culture, it is far too easy to spoil children by giving them excessive amounts of toys or clothes or by taking them to expensive places. However, it is difficult to give them too much personal attention. Instead, after spending quality time with their parents, most children become satiated and will engage in independent activities or ones that involve their siblings or peers. A related way of paying attention to children that also serves to satiate them is to affirm them by recognizing their goodness and talents.

AFFIRMING GOODNESS AND TALENTS

So far in this chapter, the discussion of the expression of parental warmth has focused on appreciating and responding to the uniqueness of a child. Such love is unconditional and conveys delight in the intrinsic qualities of an individual. Another element of warmth is affirming a child's good behavior and acknowledging the manifestation of his or her talents. Several labels can be applied to this variation: giving affirmation, approval, recognition, or praise. Still, the intent of this type of communication is the same—expressing parental warmth by responding positively to something the child has done.

Effective parents do not just discipline children for noncompliance. They also provide positive feedback when their children exhibit good behavior (Patterson, Reid, & Dishion, 1992). By noticing and commenting positively when a child has been compliant or has accomplished an assigned or self-initiated task, parents are reinforcing good behavior and assuring that it will occur again.

Affirmation is also recommended when children demonstrate their intrinsic talents or skills. Like adults, children appreciate being told that they have done a good job. Children, however, are not fooled by empty praise (Erikson, 1985). Their self-esteem is bolstered only when they receive accurate assessments of their talents and contributions. Certainly, children should be acknowledged for their less-than-successful efforts, but telling a child that he or she did well when that is plainly not the case does not engender trust. Instead, parents should try to find a positive way to assist the child in further developing his or her skills.

Even children who are naturally gifted in a particular area require a concerted effort to develop their talents. During middle childhood, the need for recognition is often played out in school or through community activities, such as sports or artistic endeavors. Parents play an important part in making sure that the resources that their children need to develop their talents are available. Equally important is the parental role of giving affirmation as the child struggles to pursue higher levels of accomplishment. The motivation for these achievements, however, should come from the child, not the parent. Otherwise, the encouragement that the parent gives will seem like coercion rather than affirmation.

A child's accomplishments, whether on the volleyball court or at the science fair, are almost always the result of hard work. Frequently, they are also the cause of tension in the home as the child struggles to meet deadlines or attempts to satisfy his or her own standards of performance. An empathetic parent will separate affirming the child's efforts from sanctioning him or her for the distress that surrounded the event. Like affection, affirmation should not be coupled with disciplinary remarks so the child does not receive mixed messages.

Similar to their need for attention, children vary in how much approval they seek. Children who are high in task persistence, like Hilary the Hard Worker, get pleasure from accomplishing goals. Still, they need to know that their parents and other caretakers recognize their achievements. In fact, it is an unusual child who does not delight in receiving frequent parental affirmation.

The importance of expressing approval and using reinforcements, both verbal and tangible, has been discussed in chapter 4. Contracts were suggested as one way to change a child's less-than-desirable repetitive behaviors into something more acceptable. Daily and weekly reinforcements were recommended because, since they involve changing habitual behaviors and interpersonal processes, the targeted goals of contracts are achieved over time. On a regular basis, affirmation coupled with an immediate reinforcement can also be an effective parenting strategy. For example, if a child finishes his or her homework before supper, a parent might say that as a result of the child's independence in completing assignments, the family will have time that evening to enjoy a favorite television program together.

Sensitive parents will also be attentive to how their affirmations of goodness are received. Otherwise, children may inadvertently misinterpret their parent's praise to mean that they should always be in the helping role. Expressing parental warmth can also entail encouraging children who are naturally compliant to be more assertive.

ENCOURAGING ASSERTIVENESS

Children who are low in negative reactivity, like Freddy the Friendly or Hilary the Hard Worker, want to please people. Sometimes that need can interfere with getting their own needs met. Picture the following scenario: Hilary the Hard Worker is attending a children's arts and crafts festival at the neighborhood community center. Hilary's mom, Mrs. Williams, is volunteering at the event. While assisting other children, Mrs. Williams notices that a number of the kids are asking Hilary to pass them supplies and to help them with their projects. Hilary is graciously responding to their requests and as a result is not making much progress on her own project.

Mrs. Williams is experiencing a parenting dilemma to which she can respond counterproductively, adequately, or optimally. On one hand, she appreciates the fact that Hilary is trying to be helpful to her friends. On the other, she is concerned that Hilary does not seem to be able to take care of herself. Instead, she is engaged in the helper role at the expense of being able to join the children as a member of their group. Mrs. Williams is likely to consider various strategies for handling the situation. If she scolds Hilary by remarking, "Hilary, what's the matter with you? I didn't bring you here so that you could help the other kids. You are supposed to be doing your own project," she is using a counterproductive response. By reacting harshly to the situation, Mrs. Williams conveys that she is critical of her daughter. Hilary is likely to be confused by her mother's statement because being helpful is an attribute that Hilary values about herself and one for which she usually gets positive reinforcement. Even though Mrs. Williams's motivation would be to help her daughter be more assertive, Hilary is likely to feel that she is being reprimanded for her temperament.

A different strategy would be for Mrs. Williams to intervene by gently reminding the other children that Hilary needs time to work on her own project. Such a response is adequate because, although it resolves the immediate situation, it doesn't help Hilary solve her own problem by being more assertive.

One optimal parenting response might be first to help Hilary find a comfortable place to do her own art project, then to discuss the broader issue of assertiveness later at home. Mrs. Williams will need to find a quiet time and private space to discuss what happened so that Hilary doesn't feel she is being reprimanded.

Mrs. Williams: Hilary, what did you think of the arts and crafts festival at the community center?

Hilary: I liked it.

Mrs. Williams: I'm glad that you enjoyed the event, but I was concerned that you didn't get a chance to finish your project because you were helping all the other kids.

Hilary: Well, that's okay, because the other kids needed colored paper and paste to finish their pictures.

Mrs. Williams: Still, it wasn't fair to you that most of your time was spent helping them. You deserved the opportunity to work on your own project as much as they did. What do you think you could do the next time we attend the festival so that you have more time to enjoy working on your own craft project?

Mrs. Williams's challenge in this dilemma is to let Hilary know that she is not criticizing Hilary for being helpful but is concerned that her daughter's lack of assertiveness resulted in a lost opportunity to enjoy an event. In sharp contrast to the counterproductive exchange previously described, in this exchange Mrs. Williams discusses the issue in a sensitive way and uses a caring, rather than critical, tone of voice.

* ✹ *

In this chapter, a multitude of ways have been presented that demonstrate how parents can communicate to their children how much they cherish them. We will address the expression of warmth again in chapter 7, where it will be discussed from a more reciprocal perspective. The next chapter, however, returns to the topic of disciplining school-age children.

CHAPTER SIX
Disciplining School-Age Children

In chapter 4, a Child-Parent Behavior Contract was recommended for correcting your child's repetitive, annoying behaviors. By now, I hope you have used a contract and found out how powerful it can be, not only for changing your child's behavior, but also for improving the interpersonal dynamics between the two of you. Many child behavioral issues that parents deal with, however, are not repetitive but occur at random times in the course of daily life.

Alternative temperament-based strategies are more appropriate for isolated episodes of noncompliance or disrespectful behavior. Remarkably, the same strategies are applicable for children who frequently misbehave and for those who commit such infractions infrequently. In this chapter, behavior problems and their resolution are elucidated within the context of the family. Recommendations for disciplining school-age children are offered in the form of parenting strategies that take into account children's temperament. The components that support day-to-day child discipline are then described, as are their respective temperament-based disciplinary strategies. Finally, instructions for developing a discipline plan are presented.

BEHAVIOR PROBLEMS IN THE CONTEXT OF THE FAMILY

As most parents realize, children's behavior problems can take over a family unless they are deliberately handled. Effective parents give forethought to the strategies they use to manage their children's behavior. Discipline delivered in the heat of a battle is likely to be reactive and counterproductive. Carefully selected and implemented disciplinary strategies, on the other hand, teach a powerful lesson about values and behavioral expectations, and they reestablish an appropriate power balance between a parent and child. Essentially, effective disciplinary strategies relay the message "Hey, kid, I'm the one who is in charge. Do as I say," in a loving and well-thought-out way.

Children's behavior problems exist on a continuum. All children, at one time or another, are disobedient or disrespectful. Effective parents deal with these incidents of misbehavior by implementing one of the disciplinary strategies to be discussed later in this chapter. Decisive action on the part of parents prevents isolated events from progressing into more serious behavior problems.

Some children are frequently noncompliant and can be the source of a great deal of stress for their parents. Children who are high in negative reactivity, like Gregory the Grumpy, have particular difficulty complying with parental requests. Their intense and negative reaction to "life happens" situations can easily predominate and bring other family exchanges to a halt. If allowed, children who are high in negative reactivity can effectively take over control of the family. Such misbehavior is not the result of temperament. Instead, it begins with an expression of negative reactivity that is allowed to escalate into problem behavior that requires correction.

Although children who are high in negative reactivity, like Gregory the Grumpy, may be the most prone to engage in recurrent disruptive behaviors, any child, if permitted, can become consistently noncompliant. The goal of a frequently noncompliant child is to win a battle with his or her parent by not having to obey and making the parent lose control.

When a child's behavior becomes progressively worse, so that a parent feels that it is out of control, the problems are likely to be embedded in a *coercive process*—one in which the child is, in effect, using force against the parents and making an equally coercive parental response tempting. Understanding how a child learns to be coercive is an essential first step on the way to changing his or her behavior into something that is more respectful and socially competent. When aversive acts such as whining, crying, yelling, hitting, or throwing temper tantrums allow a child to get his or her own way, or if these tactics are successful in changing or stopping someone else's behavior, the child learns a critical lesson (Patterson et al., 1992). Successful incidents of such extreme behavior on the part of the child guarantee that others will follow—usually escalating in frequency and in destructiveness.

To interrupt an established coercive pattern, parents need to "shrink" the child to his or her correct size so that he or she acts appropriately. At the same time, parents need to consider carefully whether their own behavior has become coercive through counterproductive responses, especially yelling or hitting. Such responses can, at first, interrupt the child's aversive behavior, but they have serious repercussions within the family. Parents who yell or hit send two seriously wrong messages to their child. They declare that the child is so powerful that he or she can make the parents lose control. They also tell a child that, if you are angry, it is all right to hit someone. Furthermore, parents and children engaged in coercive processes disregard each other's feelings in an effort to achieve immediate gratification (Patterson et al., 1992). The ensuing battles impair the parent-child relationship. If the situation is not corrected, it also seriously compromises the child's psychological development by allowing him or her to avoid responsibility for engaging in destructive behavior.

As mentioned before, the strategies for disciplining children who are occasionally noncompliant and those who are frequently, even coercively, so are the same. Of course, a parent whose child is coercive will, at first, need to work more diligently to correct the child's behavior. In spite of these initial complications, the same three components underlie effective child discipline: limit setting, consistency, and monitoring. Like the contract, these are powerful parenting strategies, and parents who master their use will enjoy markedly improved relations with their children.

COMPONENTS OF DISCIPLINE FOR SCHOOL-AGE CHILDREN

In general, children who are compliant and well socialized have parents who have been effective in setting limits on their behavior. *Limit setting* consists of determining which behaviors are acceptable, effectively communicating that information, and enacting disciplinary consequences for violations. Based on their own values and attitudes, parents differ, to some degree, in the behaviors that they regard favorably, tolerate, and deem unacceptable. Consequently, what may be suitable in one family may not be suitable in another. Parents therefore should be cognizant of their values and explicit in communicating to their children which behaviors, upon consideration, are acceptable and which are not.

Children with some temperaments, as compared with others, are more amenable to accepting the limits that their parents set. Those who are low in negative reactivity, like Hilary the Hard Worker, are usually compliant. Ironically, children like Freddy the Friendly, who are also low in negative reactivity, may not be as compliant. Their temperament, which also includes being high in approach, propels them in their search of new experiences to test the limits that their parents set. In contrast, children like Coretta the Cautious, who is the opposite of Freddy, are not eager to seek adventures because they are low in approach (and thus high in withdrawal). However, because they are also high in negative reactivity, they may object to limit setting that involves familiar situations such as bedtimes or telephone use. Children whose temperament is like that of Gregory the Grumpy are likely to be rather vocal about their objections to the limits that their parents set.

Compliance with limit setting is enhanced when there is *consistency*. Ideally, the rules with which children are asked to comply and the disciplinary strategies that caregivers use should be consistent from day to day, location to location, and across various caregivers. Children who encounter inconsistencies among their caregivers are likely to be confused, or they may attempt to take advantage of the situation by playing one adult against another. The circumstances are particularly complicated in blended families, in which children may be expected to follow two different sets of rules accompanied by an assortment of consequences, depending on whose home they are in. Grandparents or other child care providers may further complicate the matter.

Negotiation among these various adults can reduce some of the discrepancies and is highly recommended. Such discussion should occur in private and involve as many of the relevant adults as possible. The first goal of the discussion should be to identify differences in rules and in disciplinary strategies. The second should be to determine whether any compromises can be made that could enhance disciplinary consistency. Although consensus among all the caregivers is the ideal, a more realistic solution is for the behavioral expectations to be so clearly stated that the child knows exactly what is expected of him or her in each situation.

The third component of child discipline is *monitoring,* which is intertwined with limit setting and consistency. Parents who effectively monitor their children outside the home ask their children five important questions:

1. Where are you going?

2. Who will be there?

3. What will you be doing?

4. How are you getting there, and how are you getting home?

5. What time will you be home?

Monitoring should also occur within the home but with more flexibility. School-age children who have been trustworthy should be allowed private time in their homes for reflection or other solitary activities.

In many situations, a child and parent may need to negotiate a number of things before permission to attend an event is given or denied. For example, a child may ask whether he or she may return home at 9:00 P.M., although the parent has set the usual time limit as 7:00 P.M. on regular school nights. The parent could appropriately respond that a 9:00 P.M. curfew might be acceptable on a weekend if the child is attending a special event, but that 7:00 P.M. is the rule for normal situations. Of course, as children get older, they need more independence, and negotiations with them become more complicated. Still, parents have not only the right but also the *responsibility* to have all the information they need to monitor their children's activities. It is essential to know your child's friends, their parents, and their telephone numbers.

Monitoring also includes assessing mood changes in your child. Achievement testing at school or rejection by a classmate are just two examples of circumstances that may be stressful—even emotionally devastating—for a school-age child. Parents usually find it easier to identify the distress of children who react by being aggressive than those who internalize their pain and become quiet and withdrawn (Achenbach, Howell, Quay, & Conners, 1991).

Regardless of which way your child demonstrates distress, daily communication helps to diffuse its effects. Encouraging your child to discuss the events of the day is one way to monitor his or her emotional state. Some children are reluctant to verbalize what is bothering them and will require a more concerted effort on the parent's part. Creative activities such as drawing or writing stories can be an effective communication vehicle for some children. The assistance of a professional who specializes in children's development may be necessary when children seem particularly upset and are unresponsive to parental intervention.

Children whose temperament is high in approach, like Freddy the Friendly, present their parents with a different monitoring challenge. The delightful exuberance of children like Freddy, although usually well intentioned, can impair their judgment. For example, Freddy's parents may have instructed him not to cross the busy intersection in front of their house unless an adult is with him. Still, Freddy might find a playground filled with his friends across the street too tempting to resist. As with all instances of disobedience, Freddy's parents need to be prepared to handle his noncompliance.

DISCIPLINARY STRATEGIES

Effective parents have a repertoire of temperament-based strategies that they use consistently to set limits and monitor their children's activities: Your style of communication can contribute greatly to your success. Keep your directives to your child short and simple, especially when he or she has been noncompliant. State clearly what you want the child to do or not do, making one request at a time if your child cannot handle complex instructions. Your instructions should be stated decisively and with good voice control. An irritable response, which is counterproductive, indicates that you are not in control of the situation. Instead, calmly and deliberately make *adequate* responses, and realize that your delivery may need to be altered based on your child's temperament. Children who are high in negative reactivity, like Gregory the Grumpy, often require a firmer response than those who are low in negative reactivity. Conversely, children who have a tendency to withdraw, like Coretta the Cautious, may do so if the parent's voice is too intense. In other words, what may appear to be an appropriately firm instruction for a child like Gregory might be intimidating to Coretta. On the other hand, a gentle request that might be effective with Coretta may not even register with Gregory.

If you make a request and do not get compliance, give *one* reminder or use the signal that you developed in chapter 3. If there is no result, take action by implementing another disciplinary strategy. Remember that issuing additional reminders or repeating the signal is counterproductive because it becomes nagging. Likewise, if you threaten your child with some negative consequence but do not follow through, you have inadvertently reinforced his or her misbehavior. An excellent disciplinary strategy for school-age children who have not responded to the limits that you have set is the loss of a privilege. Surprisingly, the lost privilege can be a minor one, as in the examples listed in Table 6, and still be effective.

There are several reasons why a lost privilege can be relatively small and still be effective. Discipline is primarily symbolic. Rather than punishing a child, discipline simply lets the child know that the parent is the one in charge. School-age children have a limited understanding of time. Consequently, a disciplinary strategy that goes on for an extended length of time ceases to be effective because the child has probably forgotten how the misbehavior was related to the lost privilege. An extended disciplinary tactic creates another problem: A child's behavior might, after the infraction, be exemplary (or at least commendable), but he or she is essentially in "debtor's prison," without a way to rectify the situation.

An important distinction exists between discipline, which sets limits and socializes a child, and harsh punishment, which has the potential to be psychologically harmful. Disciplinary strategies get their point across in an intentional way but are also related to the child's developmental level and to the seriousness of the infraction. Harsh punishment, on the other hand, is excessive and retaliatory. It is likely to cause the child to feel shame or to find a way to retaliate against his or her parents by being disrespectful or by acting out again. Table 7 gives examples of harsh punishments, which should not be used.

Another effective disciplinary strategy is to allow the *natural consequences* of the misbehavior to occur. For example, if a child is asked to put his or her dirty clothes in the hamper but does not, the natural consequence would be not having a favorite shirt be clean on Saturday when the child wants to wear it. The parent should not delay family plans so that the shirt can be washed in the morning but should matter-of-factly point out that if the child had been compliant, the shirt would have been ready because everything in the hamper was washed the night before. Instead, the child will have to select a substitute shirt for the day. Letting the natural consequences occur can be a very powerful management strategy, but a parent must always use good judgment on when to use it. Sometimes a natural consequence can be devastating to a child and thus become harsh punishment, in which case it is not an appropriate strategy. Letting a child get hurt because he or she is attempting to jump from a dangerous height is an obvious example.

Time-out is another effective disciplinary strategy intended to interrupt a disruptive event that is under way. If you are going to use time-out as a disciplinary strategy, pick a quiet, safe location for it in your home. While in time-out, your child should not have access to toys or other attractive distractions. Use the same place consistently so that he or she knows where to go when you say,

---

TABLE 6
Developmentally Appropriate Loss of Privileges

- Loss of a favorite television show for one night
- Taking away a toy for two days
- No dessert the evening the child is noncompliant
- Time-out for a few minutes in a quiet area
- No phone calls for an evening

"Go to time-out." The appropriate duration of time-out is related to your child's age—usually one minute per year is the right amount. So, if your child is six years old, time-out should be only six minutes long. Using a timer helps your child understand the length of the time-out and diminishes the chance of a power struggle between the two of you. Calmly set the timer, and tell your child that he or she can leave time-out when it rings. Remember that once the child has completed time-out, the incident is over. Do not lecture or nag the child about whatever occurred that led to the time-out.

Be forewarned that because temperament figures heavily into the dynamics, time-out does not work for all children. Some high-maintenance children cannot settle down while in time-out but only get more upset. Many children who are social and eager to try adapt so quickly that they actually enjoy time-out! And some children who have low task persistence use time-out as an escape from whatever else they were supposed to do.

DEVELOPING A DISCIPLINE PLAN

Now that you have considered a number of disciplinary strategies, use Parenting Exercise 6, on page 76, to help you formulate your plan. Think of a discipline plan as a ladder with a different management strategy on each rung, with the simplest strategy on the lowest. Ideally, parents should exert the least amount of authority necessary to redirect their children's behavior. Therefore, when you are using the plan, go up the ladder only as far as necessary, advancing to the higher steps and more involved disciplinary strategies only when the simpler ones have not been effective.

The selection of strategies should be based on the age and temperament of your child. Use the signal that you developed in chapter 3 as the first step. Or, if you are uncomfortable using a signal, give *one*, and only one, verbal reminder. If the misbehavior is not curtailed by the first step, then initiate your usual management strategy. Select a different strategy for infractions that occur inside

---

Table 7
Harsh Punishments

- Canceling an important event like the child's birthday party or a major family holiday celebration
- Denying a child a meal
- Taking away a special toy for a month
- Hitting the child

---

the home and those that happen elsewhere. For example, time-out may be effective at home but may be impractical in the car or at the mall. Finally, in those rare instances that the problem has not been rectified by your taking the second step, use the "big one." The intent of using a more severe punishment is to let your child know that his or her behavioral infraction will not be tolerated. Consequently, you have selected a punishment that matches the severity of the offense. Examples include losing, for a week, privileges such as the phone, computer, or video games. Being grounded for the same amount of time is an alternative example. Yet another strategy is to couple the punishment with something that makes amends to the family, such as removing the trash from the garage or raking the leaves. In any case, your child should be made aware that you regard the situation seriously and that you do not expect to see such behavior again.

Parents whose child has been consistently noncompliant or who has engaged in coercive processes must be especially diligent in applying the discipline plan before consistent changes will occur in their child's behavior (Patterson et al., 1992). At the same time, they will also need to provide equal amounts of positive feedback to the child when he or she acts appropriately. This is because the parents are essentially trying to resocialize the child—a process that requires a great deal of time and patience. An enormous amount of satisfaction, however, can be gained when parents see that their child has become better behaved and is less disruptive within the family.

The purpose of designing a discipline plan is to foster your child's development, reduce family strife, and, indeed, enhance family warmth and cohesion. Rather than deciding how to handle noncompliance when it unexpectedly occurs, using preplanned disciplinary strategies simplifies this vital parental responsibility. Consequently, parents are less likely to be caught off-guard, an experience that can easily lead to harsh punishment. I once grounded my daughter, Allison, for the remaining two of her high school years. After a couple of hours, I calmed down and regretted my decision. All parents make at least occasional mistakes when disciplining their children. When you do, simply admit to your child (when you are, again, composed) that after careful reconsideration, you have decided that a less severe action will suffice as the consequence for their misbehavior. The next chapter will discuss an additional set of parenting strategies that are intended to help make family life a more pleasurable experience.

Discipline Plan

Step 1: Signal or verbal reminder (Give only once.)

_____

_____

Step 2: Usual management strategy

At home (for example, time-out for six minutes)

_____

_____

Outside the home

_____

_____

Step 3: The "big one" (Use only when the first two strategies do not work. You will not want to use this method very often. Take time to think about it before using it.)

_____

_____

If you plan to use time-out, where will it be in your home?

_____

CHAPTER SEVEN
Parents Are People, Too

One of the delights and frustrations of parenting is that once it begins, it is a never-ending process. Children of all ages have legitimate needs that caring parents know they should satisfy, even when doing so is exhausting. But parents are people, too. As such, they have their own array of needs. This chapter is an honest examination of the struggles that parents encounter in trying to meet the seemingly unending needs and requests, and the idiosyncratic desires, of their school-age children. Strategies for attending to one's own personal desires while acting responsibly in the parental role are first described. Then the specific hassles of dealing with children with various temperaments and with those related to common bothersome behaviors are explored.

Sometime during the first night of an infant's homecoming from the hospital nursery, most parents realize that their life has significantly changed. Although there are isolated stories about babies who sleep through their initial night at home, most infants require attention at the most inconvenient of times. During the first few weeks or months of parenthood, the demands of being a new parent—coupled with a desire to sustain other significant relationships and, frequently, to fulfill ongoing professional responsibilities and community commitments—can feel overwhelming.

Eventually, most babies manage to sleep through the night. Still, sleep deprivation may continue as parents incorporate the growing baby's expanding repertoire of behaviors into their daily lives. Babies rapidly evolve into toddlers, who become mobile, switch to table food, learn to talk, and, eventually, become potty trained. Each additional, albeit welcomed, developmental change requires caregivers to adapt to new demands. Family complexity escalates further with the birth of other children, professional advancement, or personal or family adversity.

By the time a child enters school, parents have navigated through a continual barrage of changes that have necessitated multiple adjustments in their schedules and that can deplete their personal and financial resources. Taking an even greater toll are the disagreements that inevitably occur between parents and children over compliance issues. Parenting is often satisfying and rewarding, but it can also be demanding and frustrating. Many parents feel guilty when they are exasperated with their children because they are unaware that the hassles they have with their school-age children are common—more accurately, are to be expected. Parents in the INSIGHTS program have told us how grateful they are because the program gives them an opportunity to hear that other well-intentioned and loving parents also grapple with their parental role. Their comments regarding this dilemma can be encapsulated into two statements: "I need a break" and "These kids are driving me crazy." Are there any parents who have not felt the same way—at least occasionally, if not more often?

NOBODY CAN BE GIVING ALL THE TIME

Although the vast majority of parents are deeply concerned about their children and do their very best to satisfy their needs, *nobody can be giving all the time*. Parents need time away from their parental responsibilities to revive themselves. Without such occasions, they are likely to be impatient with their children, exhausted, and limited in the amount of parental and life satisfaction that they experience. Personal unhappiness is not only detrimental to parents' mental health, it is also likely to reverberate throughout the family.

Situations that can adversely affect the functioning of an individual are thought to derive from two sources: major negative life changes, like a death in the family or losing one's job, or daily hassles, such as losing one's keys or feeling that there are too many things to do in a given day (Kanner, Coyne, Schaefer, & Lazarus, 1981). Surprisingly, maternal reactions to daily hassles have a more detrimental impact on the behavior of school-age children than do major life changes (McClowry et al., 1994). One of the reasons that hassles can have such a profound effect on a family is that children are particularly reactive to the mother's distress, and hassles occur on a daily or near-daily basis (Patterson, 1983). Major life changes, gratefully, occur less often. When they do occur, often mothers elicit social support.

Mothers of school-age children describe many reasons for feeling distressed by their routine responsibilities (McClowry et al., 2000). They encounter many hassles due to the multiple roles that they juggle: as parents, as spouses or significant others, in relationships with other family members (such as their own siblings and parents), and in their jobs or volunteer commitments. Time is too short for many mothers to satisfy their many and often competing demands.

Although my studies focused on mothers of school-age children, time pressures are likely to cause distress for fathers as well. Ironically, the way to deal more effectively with the multiple responsibilities we encounter as parents in our contemporary society is to take a break from them. The following section describes parenting strategies that are effective because they satisfy some of our own needs.

TIME-OUT FOR PARENTS

Chapter 6 included a discussion of time-out for children. The purpose of sending a child to time-out is to give everyone an opportunity to cool down and then to resume life from a less reactive position. Parents can impose the same strategy on themselves by using one of three types of time-out. The first two are preventive in nature, providing parents with a brief intermission from the hassles of daily life so that they can respond more effectively. The third is also intended to be preventive, but has pleasure and rejuvenation as its central goal.

Time-out before responding: A ten-second pause before you decide how you are going to respond to your child's behavior or situation. To implement this strategy, say to the child, "I need to think about this for a minute."

Major time-out for parents: Use this strategy when your child's behavior or the situation is serious enough that it requires careful thinking before you respond or when you are too angry to respond thoughtfully. To implement this strategy, say something like "I will deal with this in an hour, after I have had time to think."

Time-out for pleasure: Time dedicated to you. To implement this strategy, make arrangements so that your children will be safe during your time-out. Then give yourself an opportunity to refresh and renew yourself. Not only will you benefit, but so will your children.

MORE ABOUT TIME-OUT FOR PLEASURE

If you are a parent who takes great pride in fulfilling your commitments to your children and to your other responsibilities, you may be prone to neglecting yourself and may deny that you actually *need* a break. In our INSIGHTS program, parents complete a homework assignment to give themselves a time-out for pleasure. Ironically, although not unexpectedly, the parents who have been most responsible in completing the child-centered assignments often have the most difficulty in fulfilling this one—even when the group provides peer pressure to do so. You will struggle, too, unless I have convinced you of the value of renewing yourself for your sake, as well as for the sake of your children. Or you may be persuaded to implement a time-out for pleasure if you honestly observe yourself and recognize how often you feel hassled or tired. A time-out for pleasure is a calming time—an opportunity to put the situation in a better perspective. When taken, it can leave you feeling more poised so that you can respond more thoughtfully and be more competent in your interactions with your child. As is the case for optimal parent responses, discussed in chapter 3, your own experience is more convincing than my encouragement. Take a chance, give yourself a time-out for pleasure, and see whether you return to your parental responsibilities with a renewed sense of satisfaction.

The first step in giving yourself time-out for pleasure is identifying feasible things to do that you are likely to enjoy. Although a trip to Paris might be quite wonderful, it may be impractical. Instead, think about simple events or experiences that can give you pleasure. Because you are probably juggling multiple roles and responsibilities, you may have very little time to devote to time-out for pleasure—so you will need to plan carefully. Learn to savor whatever experiences you have to maximize their impact.

Single parents can find it particularly challenging to find time for themselves, particularly if they are the sole custodial parent. Establishing support systems is crucial but often difficult to do. The support of extended family, when available, can give single parents a break. Exchanging time-outs for pleasure with other single parents is another possibility. As a last resort, try to give yourself a few minutes of quiet time after the children are finally asleep.

Parents who have spouses or other adults in the home can take turns so that each gets an uninterrupted time-out for pleasure. Or, as an alternative, arrange for a babysitter and share an event outside the home together. Such arrangements can be rejuvenating not only for the parental role but for the spousal one as well.

The list of feasible pleasures is seemingly endless, and many can be quite inexpensive. Some of our parents have told us that an uninterrupted bath (with or without bubbles) can be renewing. Others reserve a particular type of coffee or tea for such occasions or arrange for an opportunity to listen to a favorite CD or read a novel. Meeting a friend for lunch or watching a videotape are other ways to achieve satisfaction.

Another important component of time-out for pleasure is planning the event ahead of time. Schedule it when you can have an uninterrupted period of time, even if realistically you can only count on a half hour—or even fifteen minutes. Younger children and certainly babies cannot be expected to understand a time-out for pleasure. Arrangements will have to be made for their care, or you will need to select a time when they are likely to be asleep or away from home. School-age children, however, are old enough to respect a parent's time-out. Likewise, it is good for them to learn to appreciate your need for an occasional quiet moment; to see how you enjoy simple pleasures; and to observe how such events, when intentionally planned, can renew a person.

Quick—before you get distracted by some responsibility—use Parenting Exercise 7, on page 94, to list some time-outs for pleasure that are specific to your own needs and interests. Then try one, and see what happens.

IT'S NOT EASY BEING A PARENT

Until now, this book has focused on how a child's temperament influences his or her behavior and relationships. This chapter looks at family dynamics from a slightly different perspective by examining how children can be frustrating to their parents. Granted, what is bothersome to one parent can be endearing to another, but, in all honesty, most parents are at least sometimes annoyed by their children. Strategies to keep from "going crazy" are provided in this section, along with a great deal of empathetic understanding that being a parent is not always easy.

The annoying behaviors of school-age children fall into two interrelated categories. Some are demonstrative of the child's temperament. As we have discussed, these behaviors are highly resistant to change. An attempt to change a child's temperament is frustrating for both the parent and the child. Instead, we have already discussed the importance of reframing children's consistent reactions as manifestations of their temperament and developing temperament-based strategies that are effective in gaining better compliance.

Not all annoying behaviors, however, can be attributed to a child's temperament. Even those that are can be deliberately exaggerated by the school-age child in an effort to be troublesome to his or her parents. Behaviors in this category stem from a school-age child's astute observation that because they target a particular value or expectation, specific behaviors are particularly infuriating to his or her parent (Chess & Thomas, 1999). An incident that occurred when my son, Sean, was in fifth grade illustrates this point. One day, Sean's principal called his dad at work because she had been told that one of the students had brought a real handgun to school. She began investigating the incident by checking with all the parents who had jobs that might require them to own a gun. Sean's dad was employed in the investigative field and did, indeed, own a gun that he kept at work. As a pacifist, I was offended that the principal would think that we kept a gun at home and, worse yet, allowed Sean access to it. After all, Sean was not even permitted to have play guns in our home! I requested a meeting with the principal to discuss the issue and assert my contention that she had overreacted to Sean's behavior at school and blamed him for incidents in which he was not even involved. While I was emphatically informing her that we did not keep a gun at home, one of the teachers interrupted our meeting to say that Sean was in the hallway squirting his fellow classmates with an orange squirt gun. My embarrassment exceeded my need to tell her that Sean had to have borrowed the squirt gun. Instead, I ended our meeting as quickly as I could with a promise that Sean would be properly disciplined for his hallway behavior.

Although Sean's misbehavior never reached an alarming level, it sometimes appeared to be defiantly directed toward disturbing my world order, or at least it felt that way. School-age children have the propensity to hassle their parents in a very specific way. Whether these behaviors are the direct or indirect result of a child's temperament or just a manifestation of a typical parent-child tug-of-war, maintaining one's equilibrium and sense of humor while parenting a school-age child can require a concerted effort. Children with various types of temperaments often elicit particular parental frustrations.

It's Not Easy Being a Parent of a Child Who Is High in Negative Reactivity

Children who have temperaments that are high in negative reactivity, like Gregory the Grumpy and Coretta the Cautious, can turn the simplest request into a near cataclysmic event. For example, observe this scene, in which Mr. Williams is trying to get Gregory and Hilary ready for bed. Notice that simply asking Gregory to pick up the toys triggers his negative reactivity.

Mr. Williams: Okay, kids. It's 8:30. Time to put away your toys and get ready for bed. Your mother will be home from work in a few minutes.

Gregory: Hilary's the one who took out all the toys. Why do I have to help?

Mr. Williams: Gregory, you know the family rules. Both of you are supposed to pick up the toys at bedtime.

Gregory: Well, it's not fair. I don't know why we have to pick up the stupid toys every night. We're just going to play with them again tomorrow.

Mr. Williams: I'm sure that picking up the toys every night can get pretty boring, Gregory. Can you think of anything we can do to make it more fun tonight?

Gregory: Nothing makes this job fun.

Mr. Williams: What if we make it into a race? How could we divide up the job to make it into a race?

Gregory: That's baby stuff! Why don't we just let Hilary pick up the toys? She likes it when you make up silly games.

Who would not empathize with Mr. Williams after observing that scenario? After all, Mr. Williams used an optimal response, just as this book espouses, but to no avail. Instead, Gregory tries to escalate the interaction not only by being disrespectful to Mr. Williams but by taunting his sister as well. Gregory's behavior could prompt his father to feel inadequate as a parent because his initial parenting strategies were ineffective in gaining his son's compliance. Yet the same strategies, if directed towards Hilary, would probably be successful. Even the creative approach that Mr. Williams takes by turning the household responsibility into a game fails to engage his son. Instead, Gregory focuses his efforts on getting control of the situation either by eliciting a counterproductive response from his dad or by distracting him in an effort to avoid picking up the toys.

Mr. Williams is, no doubt, frustrated by the interchange. Parenting a child who is high in negative reactivity is hard work. My daughter, Allison's, temperament is cautious/slow to warm up, and she was therefore high in negative reactivity as a child. Her level of negative reactivity, however, was mild compared with her best friend, Abigail's, who was also a cautious/slow-to-warm-up child. Abigail was more than Allison's friend. Her family and ours have operated as extended families since the time that she and Allison played together in a playpen. Consequently, I have had many opportunities to observe and interact with Abigail for nearly three decades.

Although my children may have provided me with a personal impetus for learning about children's temperament, it was Abigail who inspired my professional curiosity. Repeatedly, I watched her parents patiently and sensitively interact with her. They were also clear and consistent in implementing their family rules. The very same parental strategies that were effective with Abigail's brother often met with loud resistance from her. I, too, frequently felt angry and inadequate when interacting with Abigail. No situation seemed too benign to elicit her expression of negative reactivity: selecting a movie to view, shopping for a new outfit, getting packed for a family vacation, etc., etc., etc. Today, as an adult, Abigail is a happily married woman who enjoys parenting her own children and is successful in her chosen profession. Still, those of us who loved and cared for her when she was a child remember her childhood as intense.

If you have a child who is high in negative reactivity, understand that such children by their very nature are challenging to manage—even by the most skillful of parents. Although there is nothing that can be done to change the child's temperament, there is a great deal that can be done to minimize its impact on you and the rest of the family. Just acknowledging the inherent and consistent difficulties of dealing with a child with high negative reactivity is likely to lessen your own reactivity. Table 8 includes some additional suggestions.

It's Not Easy Being a Parent of a Child Who Is Low in Task Persistence

Being a parent of a child who is low in task persistence isn't always easy, either. Such children defy organization, a characteristic that in turn complicates a parent's own life. For example, daily homework

---

TABLE 8
Strategies for Dealing with a Child Who Is High in Negative Reactivity

- A child who is high in negative reactivity cannot be remade into a sunny person, so do not even try.
- Giving too much attention to the child's negative reactivity reinforces it and convinces the child that negative reactivity is a powerful tool for controlling other people.
- Briefly and calmly acknowledge the child's reason for distress. Then redirect the conversation towards something more positive.
- Ignoring is often the best strategy for subsequent expressions of negative reactivity.
- Obedience can still be expected even if it is accompanied by an expression of negative reactivity. Focus on gaining the child's compliance while ignoring his or her attitude. This can best be accomplished by concentrating on the issue, not on the child's expressions of dissatisfaction.
- As a parent, you have the right to expect respectful behavior from your child. Be clear about the types of verbal or nonverbal expressions that are not acceptable in your home, regardless of a child's temperament.
- Mutual support from other caregivers, as opposed to blaming each other, helps to reduce parental frustrations.
- All three types of time-out for parents are essential for parents who have a child who is high in negative reactivity.

---

can become a nightmare and turn routine family evenings into chaos. Children who are low in task persistence often neglect to write down their homework assignments while at school. As a result, they may be unsure of what they are supposed to do during their designated homework time. Or they might forget to bring home the necessary materials, like worksheets or textbooks. When they do bring home materials, they get distracted while attempting to complete the work and require frequent reminders. Do I even need to describe how getting the completed assignment back to school is yet another challenge?

Parents are likely to experience similar hassles with these children regarding household responsibilities or routines. Such children frequently leave a trail of toys and supplies as they switch from one activity to another. Or a family member may not be able to find an item he or she needs because the child who is low in task persistence never returned it to its designated location.

A parent's effort to organize a child who is low in task persistence can easily result in struggles between the two of them. Having a child who is low in task persistence is particularly taxing for parents who are, themselves, high in the attribute (Chess & Thomas, 1999). Still, children who are low in task persistence perform better if their home is organized and their caregivers are consistent and realistic in their expectations. Otherwise, their tendency to be disorganized becomes even worse. Table 9 gives some other suggestions.

It's Not Easy Being a Parent of a Child Who Is High in Activity

Children who are high in motor activity, like Gregory the Grumpy, seem to be in motion all of the time. Even when they are supposed to be sitting still, they manage to wiggle or bounce. Their high energy cannot be restrained. Unless adequate opportunities exist for the child to expend his or her motor activity in appropriate ways, it will bubble over into situations that are likely to be problematic—for example, during quiet classroom times or the middle of a family dinner.

At first glance, an obvious solution would be to provide an adequate amount of sports-related activities so that the child's high activity has a suitable outlet. Keeping up with the schedule and movements of highly active children, however, can certainly tax a parent with a normal energy level, even one who is unusually energetic. Well-intentioned efforts on the part of parents to satisfy all the desires of their high-activity children may not be possible without depleting their own energy. Instead, the needs of all the family members must be considered and decisions made accordingly.

Fortunately, time tends to reduce the hassles involved in having a child with high activity. As children get older, their motor activity tends to become more directed (McClowry, 1995a). Simultaneously, they can negotiate more of their activities within the community independently. Eventually, if you are very, very, patient, they learn to drive a car or to navigate public transportation on their own.

It's Not Easy Being a Parent of a Child Who Is High Maintenance

The discussion in chapter 2 about the child who as a high-maintenance temperament acknowledges that it is not easy being high maintenance. Many of the children in the INSIGHTS program, who were as young as six years of age and who had that type of temperament, were able to describe their own tendencies to be high in negative reactivity, low in task persistence, and high in activity. They were also aware that they had interpersonal struggles that others did not appear to have as often. The distress that these children experience is not theirs alone but reverberates among those who deal with them. Parents of children with high-maintenance temperaments, compared with those whose children are more like the other three profiles, report having the most problems managing their children's behavior.

TABLE 9
Strategies for Dealing with a Child Who Is Low in Task Persistence

- Be sure that you have made eye contact with your child and that he or she is attentive before you engage in a conversation.

- Determine which situations require the child who is low in task persistence to complete a responsibility versus those that are inconsequential.

- Provide opportunities for play or rest after concentrated periods, such as immediately after school.

- Divide complicated responsibilities or assignments into smaller, more manageable components.

- Immediately acknowledge your child when he or she has completed a component. Then move onto the next one or, if necessary, provide a brief break between components.

- Consider using a timer so your child knows how long he or she is required to work on the assigned tasks.

- Use behavior contracts. Children who are low in task persistence respond well to behavior contracts because well-written ones include manageable goals and built-in reinforcements (see chapter 4).

- Keep in close contact with your child's teacher regarding school and homework assignments. Better yet, include the teacher in your child's behavior contract.

- Although children who are low in task persistence need their parents to provide consistency and structure, do not expect your child to be grateful, especially if he or she is also high in negative reactivity.

- If your child has a choice of assignments, assist the child in selecting one that he or she finds interesting. (This provides further motivation.)

- Encourage activities that foster sustained concentration (like chess or other board games) rather than those that foster quick reactions (like video games).

- To reduce some of the hassle factor, develop an appreciation for creativity. Take time to observe whether your child's divergent thinking and unique approaches to situations lead to outcomes that might otherwise have been missed had he or she taken a direct and organized path.

The interpersonal problems of children with high-maintenance profiles are not restricted to their parents. Sibling dyads that include one high-maintenance child are likely to engage in negative interactions such as quarreling and fighting (Brody, Stoneman, & Burke, 1987). Difficulties with peers and in accommodating to classroom routines are also evident.

If you have a child whose temperament is high maintenance, acknowledge to yourself (but not to your child) that his or her behavior can often be difficult to manage, a situation that can be distressing to you. Table 10 lists some other parenting strategies to use with these children.

Frequently, parents, teachers, and clinicians ask the members of our INSIGHTS team whether there is overlap between children who are high maintenance and those who are diagnosed as having Attention Deficit Hyperactivity Disorder (ADHD). On a definitional level, there appear to be similarities. The symptoms of ADHD include developmentally inappropriate levels of attention, concentration, activity, distractibility, and impulsivity. These impairments occur across multiple settings such as home, school, and within peer relationships (National Institutes of Health, 2000). Remarkably, although there has been a great deal of research on child temperament and on ADHD, little research has been done to examine the similarities and differences between these two perspectives on children's behavior.

Despite an impressive amount of research, controversies about ADHD continue to exist regarding its diagnosis and treatment, particularly regarding the use of prescribed psychostimulants. Consequently, many parents continue to struggle with deciding whether their child should be evaluated and treated for ADHD. On the one hand, without a medical diagnosis of ADHD, children exhibiting disruptive behaviors that are interfering with their lives are unlikely to qualify for insurance coverage, nor are they likely to have full access to professional evaluations and treatments, such as medications and/or special school resources, including behavioral management. On the other hand, although medication has been shown to reduce the symptoms of ADHD for many, it is not effective for every child. In the largest and most definitive study done to date, medication combined with behavioral intervention was found to be most effective, particularly when parents improved their disciplinary strategies during the course of treatment (Jensen et al., 1997).

In contrast, the temperament field has a long history of regarding children's individual differences as existing along a continuum, without attaching a diagnosis that suggests that a child is disordered. Instead, the environment is examined to see whether it provides "goodness of fit" (see chapter 1; Carey, 1997; Chess, 1960). For example, a child whose temperament is high in negative reactivity, low in task persistence, and high in activity is likely to be stressed in the vast majority of classrooms in the United States, where the expectation is that children remain quietly and pleasantly engaged while maintaining their concentration for extended periods of time. As a result, many children are temperamentally disadvantaged in the typical classroom and may demonstrate their distress in a variety of ways (Jensen et al., 1997; Martin, 1994). Ironically, when viewed from an evolutionary viewpoint, the same type of individuals may have been advantaged in primitive society because survival necessitated hypervigilence, rapid scanning, and

TABLE 10
Strategies for Dealing with a Child Who Is High Maintenance

- Acknowledge that no parent should be expected to be as patient as you need to be to deal effectively with your child.

- Understand that the child who is high maintenance is likely to need you as his or her advocate. Unfortunately, this role may further increase your sense of being burdened.

- Use a combination of the strategies that have already been suggested for children who are high in negative reactivity, low in task persistence, and high in motor activity.

- Realize that child-parent contracts will need to be used for an extended period, even after your child appears to have changed a particular behavior.

- Provide generous amounts of warmth, frequent reinforcements, and affirmation for positive behavior.

quick motor activity (Jensen et al., 1997). As our society has evolved and changed, so have our behavioral expectations for children.

In the final analysis, no one knows your child and your family situation better than you. Some children's impairment is so great that medication is necessary. For many others, strategies like those presented in this book can be a first-line preventive measure or one that can be combined with other treatment modalities. In any case, recognizing your child's temperament and knowing the management strategies that work best can assist you in your advocacy role and in providing the warmth and discipline that these children need.

It's Not Easy Being a Parent of a Child Who Is High in Withdrawal

Children who are high in withdrawal can be exhausting because they need a great deal of reassurance from their parents and other caregivers. If a child is also high in negative reactivity, like Coretta the Cautious, frequent expressions of distress can strain parents' patience. Whining, crying, and other expressions of negative reactivity when encountering new situations can be annoying, especially if a parent does not understand why the child is so high in withdrawal.

Reframing is an important first step, but it may not be enough unless a parent also learns to read the subtle cues such children give when they are in need of reassurance. Children who are high in withdrawal are often very sensitive. They are astute observers of the world and of the emotions of those around them. They can react to subtle changes or situations that most individuals would not even notice. Such sensitivity can make parenting them even more of a challenge because children who are high in withdrawal may not be able to verbalize what they are experiencing. Last year my daughter, Allison, who as a child was cautious/slow to warm up (and thus high in withdrawal), described a situation she remembered when she was in first grade. She recalled that when she needed to use the bathroom during the middle of the night, her father would escort her and stay outside the room until she was finished. Then he would walk her back to her bed. However, when I got up to respond to her call, I simply turned on the bathroom light and then went back to bed. At age twenty-eight, she told me that she was still upset with me for not meeting her needs as a child for more reassurance and nurturance in the middle of the night. I told her that I was sorry but that I had not known that she had been frightened. I wish that Allison had told me at the time so I could have done more. I apparently missed the subtle cues that she needed reassurance. To appease my guilt, I bought her a lovely night light for her twenty-ninth birthday and told her it was my way of trying to apologize for my lack of sensitivity to one of her childhood needs.

Our society is particularly unsupportive of boys who are high in withdrawal. Boys are expected to be adventurous and to handle disappointments without emotional expressions of distress. Other children can be cruel to boys who are timid and may tease or taunt them, which only serves to increase their tendency to withdraw. The need for parental advocacy in such situations can further add to parents' feeling of being burdened and to these children's tendency to withdraw.

The good news is that childhood cautiousness can evolve over time so that it interferes less with life and requires less parental reassurance. In a longitudinal study of children's temperament, parents of children who were high in withdrawal who were warm and accepting and who did not push their children to be independent too soon had children who demonstrated greater social competence than children whose parents were harsh in their disciplinary practices (Prior, Sanson, Smart, & Oberklaid, 2000). Recognizing the positive side of having a child who is sensitive to the environment is another way to lessen the parental burden. Such children can be counted upon to observe things in life that the rest of us miss.

It's Not Easy Being a Parent of a Child Who Is High in Approach

One of the most troublesome concerns in parenting children who are high in approach is the constant monitoring that they require to ensure their safety. A secondary and related factor is the worry that results from their escapades. I speak from experience: My son, Sean, is high in approach. His exuberance for life, while delightful, was often a source of worry for me during his childhood. One time, our family was visiting the Museum of Science and Industry in Chicago. Sean was ten at the time and was known for wearing "sweats" everywhere he went. Because the museum visit was a special occasion, he selected his favorite sweats—the ones that were the most comfortable and obviously the most worn. In other words, he looked very relaxed and seemed to be a member of a family with extremely limited resources. While we were touring the exhibits, I noticed that there was suddenly a flurry of activity. Ropes and other barriers were erected, and security guards and other official-looking personnel with guns seemed to be everywhere. Eventually, we became aware that Barbara Bush, first lady at the time, was making an appearance to gain publicity for her family literacy program. Sean managed to break away from the rest of us and attempted to get near Mrs. Bush so he could get her autograph. Although we could see him running in and out of the barriers (he was also high in activity and moved very quickly), he was careful not to make eye contact with us because he knew that if he did we would corral him back. I was worried about the reactions of the museum's security guards and the other official-looking personnel, who were obviously secret service agents. They seemed somewhat alarmed about this small person who kept trying to get near Mrs. Bush. Finally, Sean managed to wiggle his way to her. She graciously stopped to talk to him and, while giving him an autograph, said, "I noticed that you worked really hard trying to reach me. Let this be a lesson to you—if you persist, you win."

The story has a pleasant ending because of the warmth of Barbara Bush and the tolerance and professionalism of a number of security personnel. But I will never forget my panic as I watched Sean dart in and out of their ranks. Like their prototype, Freddy the Friendly, Sean and other children who are high in approach are always on the lookout for new adventures. Our parents in the INSIGHTS program have reported that they have more problems parenting children who are social/eager to try than those who are industrious or cautious/slow to warm up. Only parents with children whose temperament is high maintenance report more problematic behavior.

About a year after the museum incident, Sean and I had a discussion in which he told me that I was frustrating him. He wanted to experience all of life but felt that I was holding him back. The rest of his childhood and adolescence required careful negotiations on both of our parts to balance his need for excitement with my need to monitor his activities and safety. Yet, in spite of these concerns, I have always appreciated his exuberance and contagious love of life.

It's Not Easy Being a Parent of Children with a Variety of Temperaments

The focus of this book has been on individual parent-child relationships. Most parents and children, however, live in more complex social organizations than just a dyadic one. Instead, they are almost always part of a larger family, both nuclear and extended. Consequently, parents may find themselves dealing with multiple children with a variety of temperaments. An ideal environment for a child with one temperament may not be as desirable for another.

Perhaps family life might be simpler if all the children in it had the same temperament—but would it be as interesting? If you have observed the dynamics of a complex organization, you will probably agree that having people with diverse temperaments is essential to maintain and advance the life and work of the group. Family life, in many ways, mirrors the interactions in small organizations. Each member has the potential to contribute something unique based on his or her temperament and talent.

Meeting the diverse temperament-related needs that occur among children can be complicated because these needs are often the source of conflict. Yet children with siblings have a wonderful opportunity to learn the complexities of relationships and family life because, invariably, siblings have a variety of needs and interests. Children with siblings can learn important relationship skills, such as taking turns and, sometimes, participating in and supporting someone else's interests. These activities can be critical later to their own success in maintaining adult relationships. In other words, the wear and tear of daily interactions with brothers and sisters prepares children for the often challenging realities that are present in intimate adult relationships.

Parenting children of diverse temperaments isn't easy if parents think that they are responsible for resolving all conflicts that exist among siblings. Not only is such a goal unrealistic, but attempts to do so rob children of critical opportunities for learning the realities of intimate relationships and group life. Of course, parents need to intervene when one child is endangering the safety or well-being of another. Minor altercations between siblings, however, are opportunities to expand children's interpersonal competency not only in controlling aggression, but also in empathy, communication, cooperation, problem solving, assertiveness, and conflict resolution (Bierman & Greenberg, 1996; Cowen, 2000). The temperaments of your various children will, of course, complicate the process. For example, children with temperaments that are low in negative reactivity may have an easier time being empathetic, but they may need assistance in assertiveness. Children high in negative reactivity may need more assistance in controlling their aggression and in being respectful of their siblings.

Teaching interpersonal skills to children is not easy for some parents because such learning occurs primarily through role modeling. Most of what parents teach their children about getting along with others and about intimacy takes place when children observe how their parents conduct themselves within the complexities of their various relationships at home, within their extended families, and in the community. In other words, parental behavior speaks much louder than discussion. Parents who are competent in their own interpersonal skills will find relaying such skills less burdensome than those who are conflicted in many of their own relationships. Parents who have difficulties in their interpersonal dealings are encouraged to get assistance in resolving such issues for their own sakes, as well as for their children's.

OTHER COMMON BOTHERSOME BEHAVIORS

Some annoying child behaviors are not related to temperament or even to social competencies but are commonly exhibited by most school-age children at one time or another. Parents in our INSIGHTS program have rated bedtime struggles as one of the most bothersome. Another frequently bothersome school-age behavior is lying (McClowry & Galehouse, 2002).

Bedtime Struggles

Preschool children comply better with an appointed bedtime when there are rituals. For example, preschoolers typically enjoy bath time, followed by a favorite story, a final drink of water, and a good night kiss with a tuck-in under the blankets. Getting school-age children to retire for the night requires more subtlety because their appropriate need for more independence interferes with many of the aforementioned rituals. Instead, parents need to create an environment in the evening that encourages children to settle down before bedtime. Otherwise, a child who is abruptly asked to go to bed while still stimulated from the evening's activities is likely to have difficulty making the transition. Table 11 lists a few other suggestions.

Lying

Another behavior that often upsets parents is lying (McClowry & Galehouse, 2002). In actuality, all children lie at one time or another. Still, parents often find lying upsetting because they feel that such behavior violates their trust. From a pragmatic viewpoint, however, it helps to recognize that younger school-age children are not intentionally lying but are trying to avoid punishment or attempting to get something that they want. Older school-age children, on the other hand, may recognize what they are doing but

---

TABLE 11

Strategies for Reducing Bedtime Hassles

- Recognize that children (and parents, too) have varying needs for sleep.
- Arrange for some quiet time in the last half hour or hour before bedtime so that children have time to settle themselves before they go to bed.
- Understand that school-age children cannot be forced to sleep but can be required to respect an established bedtime.
- Know that reading an enjoyable book (not a textbook) at bedtime is a natural way for children to relax before falling asleep.

---

would rather risk getting caught in a lie than tell their parents they have violated a rule.

Many of the same disciplinary strategies that have already been presented apply to lying as well. If you handle the situation matter-of-factly, you can turn the incident into a learning experience. Try to get your child to verbalize why he or she lied. By discussing the situation, you can help him or her to appreciate why the statement was untruthful. At the same time, the discussion can help you clarify your values and expectations for the child's behavior.

Discussing the lie with your child may not be enough to discourage such behavior in the future. To emphasize that you take the situation seriously, you may wish to discipline your child not only for having lied, but also for the misbehavior on which the lie was based. If a child lies frequently, then the problem should be handled with a Child-Parent Behavior Contract (see chapter 4).

Regardless of the disciplinary tactics that you choose to administer, be clear that you do not accept lying in your home. The best way to discourage your children from lying is by setting your own good example and by acknowledging instances in which family members demonstrate honesty.

✳ ✺ ✳

A harmonious relationship between a parent and child is not something that is achieved but is an ongoing process to which one can aspire. It is critical to recognize and satisfy the needs of the child, but that cannot occur in a vacuum. Parenting the school-age child must be viewed within the larger context of the family so that the needs of others are also respected—including those of the parents.

Time-Out for Pleasure

Some parents need to be reminded to give themselves time-outs for pleasure. Think of a few things that you can do that are pleasurable. Keep your ideas realistic, but be creative.

1. _____

2. _____

3. _____

4. _____

5. _____

Choose one of the ideas you listed, then select a particular time of the day or week for your time-out for pleasure. Write it down to remind yourself to use it.

_____

Your Child's Unique Temperament: Insights and Strategies for Responsive Parenting
© 2003 by Sandee Graham McClowry. Champaign, IL: Research Press. (800) 519–2707.

PART 3

Putting It All Together

CHAPTER EIGHT

Fostering Independence and Looking Towards the Future

Children become increasingly complex human beings during the school-age years. The physical growth that they undergo is visible, but other, more subtle developmental changes also occur. The cognitive skills of children dramatically mature during middle childhood, and their capacity for abstract thinking increases. They also gain competence in handling situations that require them to evaluate a variety of actions and to assess their likely consequences. Most children also increasingly engage in independent social activities as they advance through elementary school, giving them opportunities to develop friendships that exist outside the family unit. Simultaneously, they acquire the ability to understand the perspectives of others. Consequently, they have a greater potential to engage in mutually reciprocal and compassionate relationships. All these normal developmental processes are best facilitated by parents who appreciate that, although they are not relinquishing their control, they are helping the school-age child to transition from dependency to self-regulation (Collins, Harris, & Susman, 1995). In this chapter, we will discuss the parental role of fostering independence during middle childhood—a paradoxical process of holding your children close while letting them go.

JUST WHEN YOU THINK YOU HAVE FIGURED THEM OUT

In many contemporary as well as ancient societies, becoming seven years of age is accompanied by an expectation of more adult behaviors and responsibilities. In the United States, as contrasted with some less-developed countries, children are protected from joining the workforce but are expected to acquire the societal tools that they will need in adulthood. Reading is considered an essential skill, as is mastery of other academic subjects and the more mundane, but essential, activities of daily living. A great deal of this learning is transmitted through the educational system. Families and communities also contribute to the ever-widening world to which the school-age child is exposed. Moreover, what children learn and experience during middle childhood often creates in them a desire for more expansiveness in their lives and for progressive independence from their parents.

Earlier in this book, parenting was described as having two major components: warmth and discipline. Emanating from both of those components is another vital parental responsibility: fostering a child's independence. In some ways, encouraging a child to become increasingly self-sufficient is more complex than simply relaying warmth or using effective discipline strategies because it requires that a parent facilitate the child's ongoing maturation. Invariably, just when you think that you have figured your child out, a developmental change occurs. Some of these transformations are biologically driven, like the cognitive ones that occur as the neurological system matures. Other modifications occur when children apply their new skills. For example, you may have altered your child's behavior by using an effective parenting strategy, only to realize that he or she has selected another way to be annoying or disruptive. Or your child may have learned through trial and error to approach you in a certain way because it is more likely to result in a positive response to a request.

Another reason that fostering independence is complex is because it takes a great deal of wisdom to discern how much independence to give the child. Granting too much or too little freedom to a child can result in deleterious consequences. When prohibited from becoming self-reliant, some children remain inappropriately dependent, whereas others become resentful and defiant. On the other hand, children who are granted too much independence may feel neglected and may conclude that they are not loved. As a result, they may take advantage of their freedom and engage in risky behaviors. Other children who are not monitored may react in the opposite way by becoming overly conscientious and assuming roles and responsibilities that deny them the time and energy to enjoy their childhood. Such children may also take on a parental role with their own parents—a process that distorts family dynamics and seriously compromises the likelihood that these children will get their own needs met.

Although fostering a child's independence may be complex, it certainly can be accomplished. Some of the temperament-based parenting strategies previously discussed in this book can facilitate the process. You have already learned to recognize and respond sensitively to your child's temperament. This skill will aid you in fostering his or her independence. For example, some children are eager to be independent: If your child desires to navigate a developmentally appropriate situation alone, he or she would be best supported if you remain attentive but in the background. If, however, you have a child whose temperament is cautious, he or she will require your gentle support to negotiate the situation satisfactorily. You can also foster your child's independence by using the strategies to be discussed next.

ENHANCED PARENTING STRATEGIES: FOSTERING CHILDREN'S INDEPENDENCE

Parents of preschool children frequently use distraction or immediate sanctions to deal with child misbehavior. During middle childhood, effective parents alter the way that they manage their children by engaging in enhanced communication and disciplinary strategies that include *negotiating* and *reasoning* (Collins et al., 1995). They also assist their school-age children in *planning ahead*. We begin an exploration of these strategies with their definitions.

> **Negotiating:** A process between a parent and child through which a mutual agreement or a compromise is achieved.

> **Reasoning:** A strategy initiated by a parent to help a child understand the probable consequences of a particular action.

> **Planning ahead:** A discussion with a child that is intended to help him or her anticipate and organize what is needed for an upcoming event or situation.

In some ways, the enhanced strategies that foster a child's independence are similar to optimal parental responses, first defined in chapter 3. Like optimal parental responses, these enhanced strategies acknowledge the individuality of your child and help him or her mature. In contrast, counterproductive parental responses do not foster a child's independence but instead elicit immature behavior.

Other comparisons with previously discussed strategies can be made. In chapter 4, Child-Parent Behavior Contracts were recommended for repetitive behavior problems. Negotiations are analogous to these behavior contracts because they actively engage your child in the problem-solving process. However, rather than resulting in a written contract, negotiations result in a verbal agreement. Likewise, similar to the disciplinary plan presented in chapter 6, negotiating and reasoning communicate your expectations for appropriate behavior. The difference is, whereas a disciplinary plan is intended to handle isolated episodes of disobedience or disrespectful behavior, negotiations and reasoning are more complex and engage your child in thinking sequentially about his or her actions and considering their possible consequences.

Although the enhanced strategies to foster independence have been defined separately, they often are implemented simultaneously, as the following two scenarios demonstrate. In the first, Coretta the Cautious and her mother are discussing a Child-Parent Behavior Contract that they have implemented.

Tragedy Occurs at Hefty Burger

Ms. Lewis: Congratulations, Coretta. By finishing your daily reading assignment today, you earned another sticker. That means that you got twelve out of fourteen possible stickers during the two-week period that we agreed to have a behavior contract. Good work!

Coretta: Can we go to Hefty Burger for lunch so that I can get the kid's meal you promised I could have if I got enough stickers?

Ms. Lewis: Well, it is time for lunch. Should we go now?

Coretta: Let's go. I can't wait to get Lady Susan from the Planet Oringo. She comes in the kid's meal box.

(Coretta and her mother happily go to Hefty Burger—unaware that tragedy is about to strike.)

Ms. Lewis: We'll have one burger and a large cherry drink and one kid's meal with a Lady Susan.

Counter-person: We don't have any more Lady Susans. We have Prince James, Tommikins, or Pronto Robot. Which one do you want?

Coretta: But, Mom, you said I could have a Lady Susan. I worked really hard to get a Lady Susan, and you promised me. I want Lady Susan.

One of the hardest lessons for children to learn is that life is not always fair. After all, Coretta had fulfilled her part of the contract, and her mother certainly intended to keep her promise in getting the agreed-upon reinforcement for her daughter. Neither Coretta nor Ms. Lewis, however, anticipated that Hefty Burger might fail to have enough Lady Susans available. The dilemma is an example of one of those "life happens" situations that were first described in chapter 3. Here is that process again.

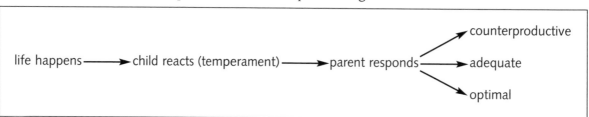

The "life happens" event in the previous scenario is that Lady Susan is sold out. Coretta responds in a way that is consistent with her temperament by exhibiting her negative reactivity. In turn, Coretta's mother might respond counterproductively, adequately, or optimally. An example of a counterproductive response would be if Ms. Lewis chastised Coretta for expressing her disappointment.

Ms. Lewis: Stop crying right now. You're always causing problems. Here's Prince James. You like him anyway. Eat your hamburger, and that's enough. I don't know what's the matter with you.

Ms. Lewis is unlikely to be as insensitive as this example suggests. Instead, she probably would use an adequate parental response, especially while they are standing in a line at Hefty Burger, a situation that does not permit time for negotiations. The following adequate parental response is likely to resolve the problem quickly and decisively.

Ms. Lewis: Let's get Prince James now. You like him, too. Then next week I'll bring you back to get Lady Susan. That way you will get two kid's meals and two characters.

To use an optimal parenting response, Coretta's mom will need to negotiate with her daughter. Since the counter-people at Hefty Burger are not known for their patience, Ms. Lewis and Coretta may need to step out of the line for a moment to discuss the situation.

Ms. Lewis: Looks like we have a problem, Coretta. What suggestions do you have for solving it?

Coretta: Why don't we go to another Hefty Burger right now?

Ms. Lewis: We can't do that today. I have to be at work in an hour, so we don't have enough time. Any other ideas?

(Ms. Lewis pauses to give Coretta an opportunity to respond. Coretta doesn't answer but becomes more upset.)

Ms. Lewis: Should we ask the man if they are expecting to get any more Lady Susans?

Coretta: Okay, but will you ask him?

Ms. Lewis: *(To the counter-person)* Are you expecting any more Lady Susans?

Counter-person: Not till next week, lady.

Coretta: Let's come back next week, Mommy. I can wait to get a Lady Susan.

Ms. Lewis: That's a good idea, Coretta. But since we're both hungry, why don't you get a kid's meal with another one of the characters now. Then next week I'll bring you back to get Lady Susan. That way you will get two kid's meals and two characters for all your hard work on the behavior contract.

In this last example, Ms. Lewis demonstrates the use of enhanced parenting strategies. First, she *negotiates* with her daughter by eliciting Coretta's suggestions for solving the dilemma. The one that Coretta offers, which is to go to another Hefty Burger, is not feasible because Ms. Lewis needs to be at work soon. In spite of the time pressures, however, Ms. Lewis continues to *reason* with her daughter by calmly explaining the situation to her. She also remains attentive to Coretta and recognizes how her temperament might influence her reaction to the disappointment. As soon as Ms. Lewis recognizes that Coretta is becoming overwhelmed by the situation (a reaction that is not unexpected, given that her daughter's temperament is high in withdrawal), she talks to the counterperson on Coretta's behalf. When Coretta comes to the decision that she is willing to wait another week so that she can get a Lady Susan, Ms. Lewis demonstrates warmth by providing her daughter with an unexpected reinforcement—a bonus kid's meal and Planet Oringo character. Although both the adequate and the optimal parenting responses result in the same number of hamburgers and characters, the processes are different. The optimal parenting response fosters Coretta's independence by engaging her in the resolution of the dilemma.

The next scenario, involving Gregory the Grumpy, demonstrates how *planning ahead* can foster a child's independence. The "life happens" situation in this case is one that Mr. Williams is trying to prevent from happening, not one that has already occurred. The circumstance that causes Mr. Williams to be concerned is Gregory's upcoming weekend camping trip with his scout friends. Mr. Williams knows that because Gregory's temperament is high maintenance, his son is unlikely to organize what he needs for the trip. Without timely parental intervention, Gregory's camping trip is likely to cause a great deal of family chaos. Instead, Mr. Williams intervenes by assisting Gregory in planning ahead.

Averting an Organizational Crisis

Mr. Williams: Hey, Gregory, isn't your big camping trip coming up soon?

Gregory: Don't worry about it, Dad. It's in two weeks, and I've got plenty of time to get everything ready.

Mr. Williams: Well, Mr. Carlson sent me a list of things that the two of us will need. I was surprised to see how much is on that list. I'm not even sure if we have everything we're going to need. Let's go to the basement and start checking. We may need to go to the sports store for a couple of things, and this would be a good weekend to do that. For example, it says that we both need sleeping bags. Let's go downstairs and see if we still have two sleeping bags.

Mr. Williams certainly does know his son. He anticipates that Gregory will not be eager to start planning ahead, and he is right.

Instead, Mr. Williams fosters Gregory's independence by prompting his son to get organized, even if it requires his step-by-step intervention. In all likelihood, planning ahead would have taken a different course for a child with an industrious temperament. If Hilary the Hard Worker had received a list of necessary supplies for one of her planned activities, she might have inventoried her home independently and then requested that Mr. Williams take her on a shopping trip for the missing supplies! Or Mr. Williams may have needed merely to suggest to Hilary that she check to see what is available in order to mobilize her to action.

When used appropriately, strategies that foster independence engender warmth and mutual respect between a parent and child. The parent relays to the child that his or her thoughts are important. The child, in turn, shows attentiveness to the parent's opinion. If the child fulfills the verbal contract he or she makes in the negotiation process, trust builds. The next time a situation arises that requires the child to decide on a suitable course of action, the parent is likely to feel more comfortable in relying on the child's judgment. There is, however, an important caveat: Even if a child has repeatedly proven to be trustworthy, monitoring is still necessary to achieve an optimal balance between parental involvement and the fostering of independence.

Enhanced parenting strategies that foster independence also assist parents in transmitting the values and culture of the family and provide children with an opportunity to internalize them. In contrast, giving stern directives may prompt children to obey, but they do so at a cost. Because they have not been prepared to think independently, children whose parents dictate strict rules for their behavior are disadvantaged when they face the dilemmas that life will invariably present to them.

Unfortunately, not all children are reasonable when negotiating with their parents. Some refuse to reach an agreement or compromise, insisting on their own demands instead. In such cases, parents need to set clear limits and reestablish their authority. Other children may reach a verbal agreement with one or both of their parents but fail to fulfill their part. Still others may not be receptive when their parents try to reason with them. In such cases, parents are encouraged to develop a relevant Child-Parent Behavior Contract and to follow a firm disciplinary plan. When the child demonstrates more mature behavior, the enhanced strategies that foster independence can be reinstated.

EVERYBODY HAS A JOB

Another way to foster children's independence is to have them take on responsibilities. Depending on the household rules and available resources, school-age children should be expected to assume some responsibility for themselves. In other words, everybody has a job within the family. Examples of tasks that are developmentally appropriate for younger school-age children include making their own beds, depositing their dirty clothes in the hamper, and selecting the clothes that they will wear the next day. Others that may or may not be feasible, depending on a child's temperament and abilities, include independently finishing homework, keeping parents informed about upcoming school or community activities, and practicing a musical instrument without parental reminders. As children advance through the elementary school years, the responsibilities that they are capable of handling can include multiple components. Instead of having one task related to self-care, such as making their beds, they can be asked to handle multistep responsibilities, such as cleaning their rooms or completing more complex school projects.

Self-care activities are highly commendable, but they do not provide children with the opportunity to contribute towards the overall family upkeep. Examples of appropriate household chores for younger school-age children include setting the dinner table, taking out the garbage, and getting the mail. Older school-age children might be able to handle more expanded family responsibilities, like caring for the family pet. (But please monitor the child so that you are sure that the pet is fed!)

Families will differ in the number and type of self-care and family maintenance responsibilities a child is expected to assume. Certainly, family resources may dictate some of these choices. Single parents with full-time jobs, but with limited budgets, may need to engage their children in more responsibilities. Parents who have household help, on the other hand, may need to make arrangements so that their children have opportunities to engage in self-care and family maintenance responsibilities.

As a child gets older, self-care and family maintenance activities need to be adjusted so that they reflect the child's growing maturity and competence. Likewise, self-care and household tasks may need to be reassigned from time to time depending on the child's and other family members' schedules.

Another part of fostering the independence of school-age children is encouraging them to engage in activities that they enjoy. No matter what the family resources, childhood responsibilities should be balanced with opportunities for play. Self-selected hobbies, sports, or special interest events provide children with occasions for personal discovery, recreation, and stress reduction. They also provide children with opportunities to socialize with friends and to experience mentorship from adults outside of the family. Such activities may stimulate lifelong avocations or may even be the building blocks for career choices. Moreover, self-selected hobbies, sports, and events help children realize the importance of leisure time and playfulness—a point of view we hope they will keep throughout their lives.

PARENT MEMORIES AND MESSAGES

One of the barriers that can impede parents from fostering their children's independence may be remnants from their own early years. The way that most of us parent our children is highly related to the way we were parented and nurtured during our own childhoods. If we are fortunate, we remember childhood as a happy time, and we recall feeling loved and cherished. It's natural for parents who have had such positive experiences in their own childhoods to try to create similar ones for their own children. Unfortunately, not everyone has pleasant memories of childhood. Even as adults, painful childhood experiences can continue to have a profound effect. For example, if our parents repetitively subjected us to negative remarks when we were children, we are likely to hear those messages play like an automatic audiotape into our adulthood. Counterproductive responses directed to us as children, like the ones that follow, can adversely affect our self-esteem and reduce the pleasure that we experience from life:

- You're not pretty.

- You're not as smart as your sister.

- Listen, young man. I am sick and tired of your behavior. I hope you have a kid just like you when you grow up.

- You're fat.

- You're not capable of doing that.

- You're lazy and will never amount to anything.

The counterproductive responses that we heard when we were children and that continue to affect us in adulthood need to be interrupted. Otherwise, we are likely to redirect similar criticisms towards our children when we engage in frustrating situations with them. Learning new parenting strategies like the ones presented in this book is one way to stop such negative remarks from being passed on to one's own children. Optimal and adequate parent responses can be substituted for the automatic and derogatory messages we might have received in our own childhoods. The pain caused by negative childhood experiences, however, may require a more concerted effort to resolve. Individual therapy may be needed to release destructive memories that can compromise current relationships, including those with our children.

Not all parental responses are counterproductive. Other parental messages, like the ones listed next, create warm memories and can provide guidance for life:

- You are a delightful person.

- You are a joy in my life.

- I love you.

- Our family is concerned about those who are less fortunate.

- It is important to be respectful of others' feelings.
- We lend support to family members and to friends when they are going through a difficult time.

Warm parental messages can foster children's independence by providing them with a sense of competence and self-worth. They also encourage children to think independently. Adolescents, particularly, need to identify the values that will guide their decision-making and lifestyle choices. Dramatic developmental changes that occur during adolescence also influence the quality of the parent-child relationship. Although a thorough explanation of adolescence is beyond the scope of this book, some discussion is warranted because adolescence plays a crucial role in the gradual process of fostering a child's independence.

ADOLESCENCE IS RIGHT AROUND THE CORNER

A common myth pertaining to adolescence is that all adolescents develop a tumultuous relationship with their parents. On the contrary, parents and adolescents who have had close relationships during the stages of infancy and childhood often maintain their positive connections during the adolescent period. Although an important developmental task of adolescence is becoming more autonomous, maintaining a close relationship with one's parents is equally conducive to positive emotional development (Bowlby, 1988). Granted, the dramatic physical and psychological changes that adolescents go through during this stage pose a whole new set of concerns for parents. Once again, parents must make adjustments in how they relate to their children in order to accommodate their ongoing developmental processes. During adolescence, probably more than at any previous stage, parents need to make a concerted effort to see the world from their children's viewpoints.

The most helpful explanation of adolescence is one that I learned a long time ago. Elkind (1967) described two concepts that dominate the perceptions and behaviors of adolescents: the *imaginary audience* and the *personal fable*. In early adolescence, young people become more concerned about what other people think about them than they did during middle childhood. Consequently, they begin to think that an imaginary audience is watching them and is preoccupied with their appearance and behavior. They also believe that their imaginary audience is as critical or as laudatory as they are towards themselves. Consequently, appearances and accomplishments are of particular importance to adolescents because they are sure that their audience is always critiquing them. For the same reasons, disappointments and failures loom incredibly large and are accompanied by shame. No wonder adolescents feel that they are under a great deal of pressure! In an effort to hide from the imaginary audience and gain some relief, adolescents begin to relish their privacy. Their private habits make them appear guarded and secretive to their parents.

The second concept Elkind describes helps to explain other adolescent behaviors. In a personal fable, the adolescent tells himself or herself that no one else has ever experienced such positive or negative emotions, particularly with such intensity. Another element of the personal fable is a sense of immortality and protection from the consequences of dangerous or threatening behavior. As the protagonists in their own personal fables, adolescents feel that, although others might suffer the consequences of irresponsible behavior, they are somehow immune to the potential outcomes of reckless driving, unprotected sex, or drug and alcohol use.

Natural consequences occurring during the course of daily life gradually transform the adolescent's thinking. The imaginary audience becomes quieter, and the personal fable is overcome by encounters with reality. Likewise, developing intimacies with friends challenges the idea that the adolescent is the only one capable of deep feelings.

Elkind did not discuss how temperament is related to these normal adolescent conceptualizations. We can, however, hypothesize that children who are high in withdrawal or low in negative reactivity may be more concerned than others about being watched by their imaginary audience. Those who are high in approach, on the other hand, are likely to be strong believers in the personal fable. Regardless of adolescents' temperament, the imaginary audience and personal fable will be experienced by all during the transitional phase between the school-age years and adulthood.

Although adolescents take particular pride in being independent (sometimes while in direct conflict with their parents), they still need parental support. Adolescents have a tendency to seek guidance or comfort at unexpected times, whenever they encounter issues that they perceive to be urgent. Being available for such unpredictable moments requires some parental creativity, especially for parents who have multiple demands on their time. To complicate matters more, such discussions are often abbreviated, and parents are in the difficult and challenging position of offering comfort or advice without appearing to intrude on the adolescent.

An effective parenting strategy during adolescence is what I call *monitoring at a distance*. The same enhanced parenting strategies discussed earlier in this chapter—negotiating, reasoning, and planning ahead—still apply, but with a new twist. During adolescence, monitoring at a distance entails the child's answering the following five questions, first presented in chapter 6:

1. Where are you going?
2. Who will be there?

3. What will you be doing?

4. How are you getting there, and how are you getting home?

5. What time will you be home?

Trust builds when the adolescent truthfully relays information in response to these five questions and then fulfills his or her agreements. Because adolescents are delightfully spontaneous, however, parents should be prepared for telephone calls requesting alternatives to the agreed-upon plans. In other words, negotiations are likely to be ongoing.

The relationship between parents and adolescents builds on the emotional foundation previously established. If the relationship has been warm and respectful during the school-age years, there is a greater likelihood that it will continue to be mutually satisfying (although perhaps at times trying) during adolescence. Thus middle childhood sets the stage for supporting children in their developmental imperative to become increasingly more self-reliant as they transition through adolescence. Assuring children that they are loved, however, begins in their infancy and continues throughout their entire lifespan.

CHAPTER NINE

A Brief Accounting
of Temperament Research

The material for this book and for the INSIGHTS program, conducted in the New York City public schools, is based not only on my own research and clinical practice, but also on an extensive body of literature on children's temperament. Included in this chapter is a brief, selected review of that literature, intended to whet the appetites of parents and professionals who are interested in learning more about the topic. The reference list may also help those who wish to explore the topic further.

The temperament field is intriguing. The topic and its relationship to other constructs are best understood within the political and cultural contexts from which they have grown. Over the course of the theory's history, several research trends have periodically emerged in the temperament field, only to lose their emphasis at other times. For example, there has been a great deal of debate regarding the role that biology and the environment play in altering the expression of temperament. This and other areas of contention remain largely unresolved in the temperament literature. None of these controversies, however, should be unexpected, given the multitude of differing disciplines that study temperament. The most recent studies, however, reveal a blurring of the disciplinary boundaries, suggesting that greater consensus is beginning to occur among temperament theorists and researchers. This chapter selectively highlights the history of temperament research and describes its current status before enumerating hopes for its future.

A HISTORICAL PERSPECTIVE ON TEMPERAMENT

The genesis of temperament theory is credited to Hippocrates, who was born in 460 B.C. The actual honor, however, probably belongs to Polybus, his son-in-law and disciple (Jouanna, 1999). Whether emanating from Hippocrates or Polybus, the first theory offered stated that human nature was composed of four humors: blood, phlegm, yellow bile, and black bile. Health, based on this theory, was achieved when the humors were proportionate. Illness resulted when one was in excess.

Several hundred years later, another physician refined the theory of humors by linking them with four temperaments (Merenda,

1999). According to Galen, who was born in 130 A.D., an individual's temperament was caused by the humor that was constitutionally dominant. *Sanguine* (blood) people were optimistic and hopeful. Those who were *melancholic* (black bile) were sad and depressed. *Choleric* (yellow bile) individuals were irascible, and those who were *phlegmatic* (phlegm) were apathetic.

The relationship between temperament and biology took a different direction in the late eighteenth century (Collins, 1999). Lavater (1775–1778/1840) published a book that included many illustrations of facial characteristics, which he associated with specific temperaments and character traits. The book was translated into several languages and published in multiple editions. Although widely read, Lavater's theory was often challenged.

Another approach to body typology and temperament was temporarily popular in the mid-twentieth century. Sheldon (1942) linked temperament with three male physiques. *Endomorphs* were usually overweight and extroverted. They had large livers and floated easily in water. *Mesomorphs* were broad, strong, and energetic. *Ectomorphs* were tall, thin introverts.

Although Sheldon's research was later disputed, the underlying principle linking body characteristics to temperament continues to this day. Halverson and Victor (1976) found that children who have a temperament that is similar to the high-maintenance profile described in this book had more minor physical anomalies than did other children. Kagan (1998b) who studied inhibited versus uninhibited children (similar to the cautious/slow-to-warm-up versus social/eager-to-try profiles) also connects biology with temperament type. In his studies, 60 percent of the inhibited children had blue eyes, whereas 60 percent of the uninhibited children had dark eyes. In addition, he found that inhibited children had more atopic allergies than did their uninhibited peers.

One of the reasons that Sheldon's work in the 1940s sparked heated debate relates to the political climate that existed during and after World War II (Kagan, 1998a). Sheldon (1942) associated body types with specific racial and ethnic groups, which he further linked with intelligence and morality. His assertion was uncomfortably close to Hitler's, who maintained that Aryans were superior and that other types of people, particularly Jews, should be exterminated. Worry that some specific temperaments would be considered desirable, whereas others would be regarded as inferior, made research on the subject too politically charged for additional investigation. The topic was, however, later revived based on a different set of psychological imperatives.

By the 1950s, the mainstream of psychology was dominated by behaviorism and psychoanalytic theory. Although dramatically diverse in their content, these two theories came to the same conclusion: No matter what type of misbehavior a child exhibited, the mother was to blame. In 1956, a husband and wife psychiatrist team, Alexander Thomas and Stella Chess, began a pioneering investigation into the individual behavioral differences of children. Called the New York Longitudinal Study (NYLS), the investigation was grounded in their extensive experience as practicing psychiatrists, and it raised doubts about the prevailing psychological perspectives. As psychiatrists, parents of four children, and keen observers of the world around them, Chess and Thomas were convinced that child adjustment was not merely the product of maternal behavior, but that a child, beginning in infancy, contributed towards his or her own development.

Along with their colleagues, Chess and Thomas began collecting data on 138 primarily white, middle- to upper-middle-class infants and their families (Thomas, Chess, Birch, Hertzig, & Korn, 1963). The study continued until the original infant subjects were in their early 30s (Chess & Thomas, 1990). When the NYLS first began, the data were derived primarily from parent interviews and from observations of the infants. As the children got older, they were also interviewed, as were their teachers. Questionnaires and other psychometric tools were introduced as the study evolved.

At first, Thomas and Chess (1977) described the individual differences of the children as *primary reaction patterns*. Later they renamed the construct *temperament*, which they equated with a child's *behavioral style*. Temperament, they said, was the *how* of behavior—different from the *what* (abilities) and the *why* (motivation). They further identified nine dimensions of temperament:

1. Activity (the motor component)
2. Rhythmicity (the predictability versus nonpredictability of biological functions)
3. Approach/withdrawal (the child's initial response to new people or situations)
4. Adaptability (the response to change imposed by others or altered situations)
5. Intensity of reaction (the energy level of response, regardless of its quality or direction)
6. Mood (the amount of pleasant, joyful, or friendly behavior)
7. Persistence (the length of time the child engages in an activity, even when confronted by obstacles)
8. Distractibility (the effectiveness of extraneous environmental stimuli in diverting the child)
9. Threshold (the amount of stimulation necessary to produce a response from the child)

Chess and Thomas also described three constellations of temperaments. The *easy* child was regular with regard to biological functions, approached new situations with moderate ease, adapted easily, and had a mild and generally positive mood. In contrast, the *difficult* child was biologically irregular, withdrew from new stimuli, adapted slowly, and had a highly intense and negative mood. *Slow-to-warm-up* children were slow to adapt but showed positive interest when they were given adequate time. They also were high in negative mood but demonstrated it with less intensity than did difficult children.

A major tenet of Chess and Thomas's conception of temperament was their "goodness of fit" concept, defined in chapter 1. Goodness of fit serves to this day as the pivotal point around which temperament-based intervention is based. The goal of such intervention is to enhance the fit between the child's temperament and the demands, expectations, and opportunities of the environment.

CONTEMPORARY TEMPERAMENT THEORY

Although Chess and Thomas's work was critical in advancing the field, researchers from a number of disciplines have also contributed to the development of contemporary temperament theory. Developmental and clinical psychologists, biologists, neuropsychologists, nurses, pediatricians, psychiatrists, and educators all have brought to the field their varying points of view and research methods. A number of the major contemporary theorists, depending on their scientific background, focus on a particular aspect of temperament. Plomin and his colleagues (Buss & Plomin, 1984; Plomin & Caspi, 1999) emphasize the genetic component; Rothbart and her colleagues (Posner & Rothbart, 2000; Rothbart & Derryberry, 1981) call attention to the way that neurocognitive processes contribute towards the development of temperament; Goldsmith and his colleagues (Goldsmith, Lemery, Aksan, & Buss, 2000) highlight the socioemotional expression of temperament; Strelau (1998) elucidates it from within a stress framework; and Carey (1997) and Bates (2001) discuss its clinical applications.

Like many other developmental theories, the current body of temperament literature demonstrates a great deal of "jingling and jangling" (Block, 1995). Readers of the literature can easily become frustrated by the jingle fallacy, which occurs when the same term is used to denote different meanings. No less exasperating is the jangle fallacy, in which different terms mean the same thing. Although a variety of definitions and theoretical perspectives have emerged, the general consensus is that temperament has a constitutional basis, is a rubric for a group of related traits, is demonstrated consistently across situations, and is not easily changed. One's expression of temperament over time, however, may be influenced and somewhat altered by the environment (Goldsmith et al., 1987; Rothbart & Bates, 1998).

Temperament is considered by many within the field to be a subconstruct of personality (or its building blocks) because it has an explicit biological foundation and a developmental orientation, and because it focuses on emotions and behavioral expression (Rothbart & Bates, 1998; Strelau, 1998). Personality, on the other hand, integrates broader social factors—including skills, attitudes, self-concept, values, habits, interests, and characteristics—that develop under the influence of culture. Still, some within the field see temperament and personality as synonymous (Costa & McCrae, 2001). The adult personality factors that are often compared with the dimensions of temperament are extroversion, agreeableness, conscientiousness, neuroticism, and openness. Major investigations are currently under way examining the overlap between personality and temperament (Kohnstamm, Halverson, Mervielde, & Havill, 1998) and comparing how parents in varying cultures describe child personality (Victor, Dent, Carter, Halverson, & Havill, 1998).

LINGERING DEBATES

Unresolved conceptual and methodological debates continue to be the impetus for many of the investigations currently being conducted. These issues are unlikely to be definitively resolved in the near future. Instead, they can be expected to stimulate more complex study designs that acknowledge temperament as complex in both its genesis and in its expression across the lifespan. For example, the biological roots of temperament continue to be studied. Zuckerman (1995) conceptualizes the inherited part of temperament as a chemical template that responds physically to environmental stimulation. In an interactive way, feedback from the environment reinforces these initial physical responses. A number of biological mechanisms—such as genetics, neurological processes, enzymes, and hormones—have been found to contribute to temperament traits (Bates & Wachs, 1994; Kagan, 1998a).

The debate surrounding the biological basis of temperament has spurred investigations regarding the stability of temperament. If temperament is largely dictated by biology rather than by the environment, it should be stable. Yet studies that have attempted to show that an individual's temperament remains the same from infancy through childhood have not produced compelling results (Rothbart & Bates, 1998). When temperament has been studied longitudinally, over several years, only weak to moderate correlations have been found, indicating that temperament changes considerably over time. A number of measurement problems, such as the unreliability of some questionnaires, have previously been blamed for the lack of stability (Kagan, 1998a). In addition, the statistical methods that have been used have been called into question because most of the analyses have been based on the average scores of children rather than taking into account individual patterns of growth that are in transaction with other factors (Halverson & Deal, 2001).

The problem of examining children's temperament devoid of their environmental context cannot be overstated. When examined as a whole, the results of studies indicate that children with extreme temperaments are less likely to change than those who are in the middle range. Likewise, children whose temperaments are high in withdrawal are more likely to have internalizing problems like depression or anxiety, whereas those who were unmanageable early on are more likely to externalize their reactions. Negative reactivity contributes to both types of reactions (Rothbart & Bates, 1998). Such generalizations, however, neglect to examine how temperament is nested within biological and environmental contexts. The reason that some children change more than others still is not definitively known, but several factors appear to be influential. One explanation that is gaining popularity is that normal biological maturation triggers various genes to be activated as a child gets older; these genes in turn elicit temperament changes. A related proposition is that temperament is not static but is altered by the environment in which the child is raised. On a physical level, the environment affects the level of stimulation of some biological processes, such as those related to the neuroendocrine systems. On a social level, parents and other caregivers are significant contributors in determining the quality of the environment and the level of stimulation it provides.

The reason that most descriptive studies of school-age children fail to address the social environment adequately concerns its complexity. Such analyses require examining at least some of the multidirectional transactions that moderate the relationship between children's temperament and various functional outcomes like behavior, adjustment, and academic success. Increasingly, more studies are incorporating such process-oriented transactions, as the following two studies illustrate. Halverson and Deal (2001) explored whether task persistence changed in children over a four-year period beginning when children were three years of age. Although there was little overall change in task persistence during the four years, this characteristic tended to increase over time, especially for those children who were from well-functioning families. The importance of the family is evident in another longitudinal study that followed children from ages seven to sixteen. Children with extreme temperaments were as well adjusted as those who had mild temperaments if their families were well-functioning (Maziade et al., 1990).

Goldsmith et al. (2000) probably best summarize the comingling of biology and the social environment in influencing the stability of temperament. They assert that temperament is not a genetically driven destiny. Instead, it directs a developmental path that is intersected by the relationships and experiences that a child encounters. Thus children with various types of temperament will respond in a variety of ways to the social environment. An elegant longitudinal study by Kochanska (1997) on the development of conscience elucidates how different combinations of parenting behaviors in transaction with various types of child temperament can lead to diverse outcomes. Although fearful children in Kochanska's study developed higher levels of conscience at faster rates than did nonfearful children, maternal discipline strategies influenced the process. The promotion of conscience in children who were fearful was more effective when their mothers used gentle discipline. Fearless children, on the other hand, did not respond as well to subtle discipline but appeared to need a greater degree of maternal responsiveness to facilitate their internalization of conscience.

The results of the Kochanska (1997) study and many of the others that she has conducted support a point frequently addressed in this book: Some children, due to their temperament, are more resistant to parental discipline than others. An additional study supports the idea that insights into a child's temperament can assist a parent in determining the combination of warmth and discipline strategies that works best for a particular child. Bates (2001) explains that a child's resistance to discipline can vary from active ignoring of directives to open defiance. He found that parents of children who were highly resistant to control were more effective if they used firm discipline strategies.

Another source of debate within the temperament field, but one that seems to be coming closer to resolution, is the number of dimensions that temperament comprises. Thomas and Chess (1977) described nine dimensions, but recent examinations have reduced these to fewer, more distinct dimensions. Although the labels attached to the dimensions by various researchers differ slightly, three dimensions have been consistently found to relate to infant temperament: distress to novelty, irritable distress, and activity level (Rothbart & Bates, 1998). Negative reactivity, task persistence, approach, and activity comprise the childhood temperament dimensions (McClowry, Halverson, & Sanson, in press). Although these dimensions seem to be the most salient, other individual differences are likely to be consistent with the major tenets of temperament and could legitimately be labeled as temperament as well (Kagan, 1998b).

The measurement of temperament is another source of ongoing controversy (Mangelsdorf, Schoppe, & Burr, 2000; Rothbart & Bates, 1998). Over the years, a variety of methods have been used, including interviews, questionnaires completed by parents (usually the mothers of the children) or teachers, self-reports, and observations. Each technique has both advantages and disadvantages. For example, parent reports on questionnaires like the SATI (see the appendix) are the most frequently used because they are easy to administer and low in cost. Proponents of parent reports assert that because parents spend a great deal of time with their children and because they observe them in a variety of situations, they are best suited to report on their temperament. Kagan (1998a), however, questions the reliability of parents, arguing that parents can be biased in their reactions to their children for a number of reasons. For example, parents might have limited knowledge of normative child development and, thus, not be adequately prepared to compare their child with others. Other sources of bias that might be reflected in the subjectivity of parent reports are the parents' own personalities and their expectations for child behavior.

The quality of some of the existing questionnaires may be another reason the longitudinal stability of temperament has been elusive. The temperament field has generated a large number of questionnaires, although some of them are of questionable value. Instruments that have not undergone rigorous psychometric development should not be used. Reviews of available instruments can assist researchers and informed consumers of the literature in assessing those that have adequate reliability and validity (Goldsmith & Rieser-Danner, 1990; Goldsmith & Rothbart, 1991; Strelau, 1998).

An alternative to using parent reports is to examine temperament through observational techniques. Studying children while they are engaged in a structured activity in a laboratory or in the home may eliminate parental bias but introduces other validity issues. Observer objectivity may be compromised by the personal biases of the coders. Or the coders may be inadequately trained in the methodology. Moreover, the length of time that children are observed may be inadequate to elicit temperamental reactions that occur infrequently or only under significantly stressful circumstances. The specific setting for the observations is also a concern. Structured laboratory observations have the advantage of taking place in a controlled situation so children's reactions can be analyzed and compared. Children in a laboratory, however, may react differently than they do in natural settings. Consequently, the information gleaned from laboratory studies can lack validity if it does not tap a child's typical temperamental reaction.

The ideal way to study temperament is to use information from multiple sources and a variety of informants, collected at many different times and across various situations. The complexity of this ideal and costly approach must, however, be acknowledged. Each source of information provides only a portion of the complete picture. Moreover, findings derived from one source may be at odds with those from another and may be difficult to reconcile. The complexity of a multimethod study may be illustrated by describing an observational protocol for understanding family dynamics: Multiple observations of each family would be necessary because each one would provide different information depending on the time of day and the type of activities in which the various members of the family are engaged. Still, a patient researcher with unlimited resources and time could eventually understand the workings of a family and its individual members. Of course, the protocol would need to be consistently repeated for each of the families in the study.

Temperament researchers remain challenged to describe the complexities under which the construct operates. Multiple types of investigations and approaches will continue to be necessary to make advances in the field. Given its resurgence over the last half decade, the field has made remarkable progress in explaining how temperament contributes to the adaptive functioning of children. Parents and clinicians can use the findings from many of the studies to understand children better and to create environments that support their optimal development.

PROMISING AREAS OF INVESTIGATION REGARDING ADAPTIVE FUNCTIONING

Many talented researchers are currently hard at work attempting to elucidate further how children with various temperaments embark on different developmental pathways, leading to more adaptive or less adaptive outcomes. This chapter is too brief to review all of them. In addition to the aforementioned researchers in the field, three others are particularly noteworthy. These researchers are discussed not only for the extensive amount of research that they have conducted, but also because the results of their studies are likely to prompt new avenues for clinical intervention.

Jan Strelau (1998, 2001), a scientist at the University of Warsaw, Poland, integrates temperament within a stress framework. An important proposition of his theory is that each individual has his or her own *optimal level of arousal*. Some are easily and negatively aroused by stress. As a result, they often feel overwhelmed. Others are distressed if the environment does not provide enough stimulation or challenges. In other words, what is too much stress for some individuals is too little for others. People who require a great deal of stimulation will alter the environment so that it more closely matches their comfort level. On the other hand, those who are easily distressed are likely to withdraw emotionally or physically to alleviate stress. When examined from a goodness-of-fit perspective, Strelau's theory supports the premise that parents need to recognize when their child is distressed and feeling overwhelmed. Based on that observation, effective parents will provide additional support as they gently assist the child in gaining mastery over the situation. Effective parenting also involves recognizing those children who are experiencing a poor fit with a particular environment because it does not provide enough challenges. Sometimes, acting-out behaviors indicate that the child is trying to create his or her own excitement to compensate for the lack of stimulation provided by the environment.

Another promising area of investigation comes from the laboratory of Mary Rothbart and her colleagues (Posner & Rothbart, 2000;

Rothbart & Derryberry, 1981) at the University of Oregon. They describe an *executive attention system* that develops in children over time. Temperament, from their perspective, includes *reactivity*, which is the strength of a child's emotional reactions (such as fear, anger, and positive affect), and *self-regulation*, which permits the child to modulate his or her response. As a child develops, the self-regulatory functions increasingly become conscious, evolving into *effortful control*. A current area of Rothbart and colleagues' work is to see whether children can be helped to strengthen their effortful control. If they can, such intervention is likely to be particularly helpful for children diagnosed with an attention-deficit disorder.

A third area of investigation focusing on adaptive functioning is being explored by Nancy Eisenberg and her colleagues (Eisenberg & Fabes, 1999; Eisenberg, Fabes, Shepard, Guthrie, Murphy, & Reiser, 1999) at Arizona State University. They report that temperament in reaction to emotionally provocative situations results in two ways of being empathic. When encountering another person's negative emotions, some individuals feel *sympathy*, which is primarily a concern about the other person. In contrast, others, particularly those high in negative reactivity, experience *personal distress*, which is self-focused and accompanied by discomfort and/or anxiety. According to the researchers, when engaged in negatively charged circumstances, such individuals were less able than the other group to shift their attention away or to problem-solve, and they continued to experience distress. Another finding has implications for parent readers of this book: School-age children were better adjusted if their parents accepted their children's negative emotions and did not impose sanctions for expressing them.

Like much of the temperament research, these three areas of investigation are descriptive, which means that the researchers observed and reported on how the temperament of individuals in transaction with the environment influences their life trajectory. No effort was made to change the observed patterns—the goal was simply to identify and report them. Nevertheless, they provide a rich scientific foundation upon which future interventions can be based.

HOPES FOR THE FUTURE

On the basis of the multitude of researchers and clinicians from various disciplines who profess it as their own, the temperament field can certainly boast that it embodies diversity. The contemporary understanding of temperament can be attributed to the sustained efforts that individuals with different backgrounds have made to bridge the identified theoretical, methodological, and clinical gaps. The richness of the current understanding of temperament would not have been possible if one narrowly defined discipline had dominated the field. Instead, the heated debates that characterize this area of research have prompted the field to traverse disciplinary boundaries to generate the existing body of knowledge.

Speculating about the future of temperament research is a risky venture. As evident from its history, political and cultural events will intervene and provide directives for future research and clinical applications. Expressing hopes for the future is a more appropriate undertaking. Hopes for the future of temperament research are twofold: unrelentingly rigorous scientific investigations and improved strategies for temperament-based intervention.

It is hoped that temperament studies in the future will continue the existing trend towards incorporating contextual issues within their designs. To do this, more longitudinal studies are needed to examine how temperament is in constant transaction with the biological and social environments. Cross-cultural studies conducted in the United States and other countries will be vital in identifying similarities and differences in these developmental trajectories. Studies will also need to explore how temperament is related to other related constructs, such as motivation and intelligence (Wachs, 1999). All of these types of studies will require statistical methods that demonstrate individual growth patterns rather than just describe group changes (Halverson & Deal, 2001).

The challenges awaiting those who focus on temperament-based intervention are equally complex because they require standards as rigorous as those for the rest of the field. Once exposed to the idea of temperament, parents and clinicians alike are often interested in putting the theory and research findings to work. Parents are eager to see whether their knowledge will enhance their relationships with their children and foster their development. Clinicians wish to know how to use it to advise parents and other caregivers on child-related problems or developmental issues. The application of temperament research to clinical practice is a complicated task and should involve professional preparation. Clinicians who apply temperament theory to their work with families should be adequately trained and supervised (McClowry, 1998). Parents using temperament-based services are encouraged to ask clinicians about their educational and professional training. Likewise, the temperament field has an obligation to develop more professional training programs that better prepare clinicians for this role.

A related responsibility in the field is to assess the effectiveness of temperament-based intervention. Between 1984 and 1987, about 60 percent of the published articles reported correlational results that could be relevant to intervention because they focused on attachment, adjustment, or behavior problems (Bates, 1989). A tally from that date until March 2002 indicates that the trend continues, although there is an explosion in the number of articles. Between 1984 and 1987, 157 reports were published. The number increased to 880 in the following four years.

Although a great deal of interest exists in applying a temperament framework to real-life situations, only a few researchers are conducting studies that test the effectiveness of temperament-based interventions (McClowry, 1998). It is hoped that more energy and resources within the field will be devoted to such studies in the future.

The final hope is directed towards the multiple constituents who are interested in temperament: consumers of temperament research and interventions such as parents and teachers; clinicians, who incorporate the knowledge into their work; interventionists, who test the effectiveness of temperament-based programs; and researchers, who provide the scientific foundation. An invitation is extended to enhance the communication among these constituent groups. Such an aspiration should not be daunting for a field that has a long tradition of celebrating its diversity.

In summary, the history of the temperament field extends back to ancient times. The majority of research, however, has been conducted during the last fifty years. The contemporary understanding of temperament is broad and attests to the complexities of studying individual children within the contexts of their environments. Still, the field has provided an enormous amount of information, which forms the scientific foundation for temperament-based intervention. Future advances in temperament-based intervention will further assist parents and clinicians in supporting the adaptive functioning of children.

School-Age Temperament Inventory

The School-Age Temperament Inventory (SATI) is a 38-item parent report of children's temperament that has undergone extensive development and evaluation. The impetus for developing the questionnaire was my concern about the high intercorrelations among the nine temperament dimensions identified by Chess and Thomas (1984). I regarded these high intercorrelations as not only a statistical problem, but a theoretical and clinical one as well. I found that unless I had a list of the definitions of the dimensions as described by Chess and Thomas in front of me, I could not distinguish between some of them. In addition, dealing with nine dimensions was cumbersome when I tried to explain a child's temperament to his or her parents. I wondered whether fewer dimensions would be more parsimonious.

With two other temperament researchers, I conducted a factor analysis using three data sets (McClowry, Hegvik, & Teglasi, 1993). Factor analysis, often conducted in temperament research, is a combination of statistical techniques that examines the interrelationships among variables (Nunnally & Bernstein, 1994). The factors are then examined to see what constructs or dimensions they describe.

The results of our analysis supported the idea that there were indeed fewer than nine dimensions. Soon after, I wrote and received a grant from the National Institute of Nursing Research to develop the SATI. The four dimensions discussed in this book—activity, approach/withdrawal, task persistence, and negative reactivity—were supported by another factor analysis (McClowry, 1995c). The reliability and validity of the SATI were further tested and supported with data from parents in Connecticut, Georgia, and Australia (McClowry et al., in press). Since then, the SATI has been translated into several languages and is used by investigators around the world.

SCHOOL-AGE TEMPERAMENT INVENTORY
Directions for Completing and Scoring

Follow these four steps to produce a Temperament Profile for your child:

Step 1: Fill out the inventory.

Step 2: Transfer your answers to the Scoring Sheet.

Step 3: Use the Calculation Sheet to average the scores in relation to the four temperament dimensions, as explained.

Step 4: Transfer the scores to the Temperament Profile. Your child's salient dimensions are those in the boxes where circles or triangles appear. Boxes with circles usually suggest challenging behaviors on your child's part. Boxes with triangles indicate behaviors that parents usually consider easy.

You can also generate a Temperament Profile for your child by logging on to **www.nyu.edu/education/nursing/insights/** then selecting "Online Temperament Profile" and following the instructions there.

School-Age Temperament Inventory

Using the scale below, circle the number that shows how often your child's behavior is like the behavior described in each item.

1	2	3	4	5
Never	Rarely	Half the time	Frequently	Always

	Never	Rarely	Half the time	Frequently	Always
1. Walks quietly in the house when moving from room to room.	1	2	3	4	5
2. Gets upset when he/she can't find something.	1	2	3	4	5
3. Approaches children his/her age even when he/she doesn't know them.	1	2	3	4	5
4. Switches from one activity to another before finishing the first.	1	2	3	4	5
5. When he/she disagrees, speaks in a quiet and calm manner.	1	2	3	4	5
6. Returns to responsibilities (homework, chores) after friends call or visit.	1	2	3	4	5
7. Smiles or laughs with new adult visitors at home.	1	2	3	4	5
8. Does not complete homework unless reminders are given.	1	2	3	4	5
9. Is shy with adults he/she doesn't know.	1	2	3	4	5
10. Gets mad even when mildly criticized.	1	2	3	4	5
11. Leaves own projects unfinished (drawings, models, crafts, etc.).	1	2	3	4	5
12. Seems nervous or anxious in new situations (visiting relatives, interacting with new playmates).	1	2	3	4	5
13. Runs when entering or leaving the house.	1	2	3	4	5
14. Reacts strongly (cries or complains loudly) to a disappointment or failure.	1	2	3	4	5
15. Gets very frustrated with projects and quits.	1	2	3	4	5
16. Remembers to do homework without being reminded.	1	2	3	4	5
17. Gets angry when teased.	1	2	3	4	5

Page 1 of 2

Your Child's Unique Temperament: Insights and Strategies for Responsive Parenting
© 2003 by Sandee Graham McClowry. Champaign, IL: Research Press. (800) 519–2707.

	Never	Rarely	Half the time	Frequently	Always

18. Quits routine household chores before finished.   1 2 3 4 5

19. Bursts loudly into the room when entering.   1 2 3 4 5

20. Gets very frustrated when he/she makes a mistake.   1 2 3 4 5

21. When meeting new children, acts bashful.   1 2 3 4 5

22. Stays with homework until finished.   1 2 3 4 5

23. When angry, yells or snaps at others.   1 2 3 4 5

24. Runs or jumps when going up or down stairs.   1 2 3 4 5

25. Goes back to the task at hand (chore, housework, etc.) after an interruption.   1 2 3 4 5

26. Moody when corrected for misbehavior.   1 2 3 4 5

27. Moves right into a new place (store, theater, playground).   1 2 3 4 5

28. Runs to get where he/she wants to go.   1 2 3 4 5

29. Responds intensely to disapproval (shouts, cries, etc.).   1 2 3 4 5

30. Has difficulty completing assignments (homework, chores, etc.).   1 2 3 4 5

31. Prefers to play with someone he/she already knows rather than meeting someone new.   1 2 3 4 5

32. Makes loud noises when angry (slams doors, bangs objects, shouts, etc.).   1 2 3 4 5

33. Gets upset when there is a change in plans.   1 2 3 4 5

34. Avoids (stays away from, doesn't talk to) new guests or visitors in the home.   1 2 3 4 5

35. Seems to be in a big hurry most of the time.   1 2 3 4 5

36. When an activity is difficult, gives up easily.   1 2 3 4 5

37. Has off days when he/she is moody or cranky.   1 2 3 4 5

38. Seems uncomfortable when at someone's house for the first time.   1 2 3 4 5

Page 2 of 2

Scoring Sheet

Transfer your answers on the inventory to this Scoring Sheet. To do so, circle the number on this sheet that appears in the same column as your response on the inventory. For example:

Item 1 from the inventory

1. Walks quietly in the house when moving from room to room. 1 ② 3 4 5

Item 1 from the Scoring Sheet

1. Walks quietly in the house when moving from room to room. 5 ④ 3 2 1

✳✳✳

1. Walks quietly in the house when moving from room to room. 5 4 3 2 1

2. Gets upset when he/she can't find something. 1 2 3 4 5

3. Approaches children his/her age even when he/she doesn't know them. 5 4 3 2 1

4. Switches from one activity to another before finishing the first. 5 4 3 2 1

5. When he/she disagrees, speaks in a quiet and calm manner. 5 4 3 2 1

6. Returns to responsibilities (homework, chores) after friends call or visit. 1 2 3 4 5

7. Smiles or laughs with new adult visitors at home. 5 4 3 2 1

8. Does not complete homework unless reminders are given. 5 4 3 2 1

9. Is shy with adults he/she doesn't know. 1 2 3 4 5

10. Gets mad even when mildly criticized. 1 2 3 4 5

11. Leaves own projects unfinished (drawings, models, crafts, etc.). 5 4 3 2 1

12. Seems nervous or anxious in new situations (visiting relatives, interacting with new playmates). 1 2 3 4 5

13. Runs when entering or leaving the house. 1 2 3 4 5

14. Reacts strongly (cries or complains loudly) to a disappointment or failure. 1 2 3 4 5

15. Gets very frustrated with projects and quits. 5 4 3 2 1

Page 1 of 2

16. Remembers to do homework without being reminded.   1 2 3 4 5

17. Gets angry when teased.   1 2 3 4 5

18. Quits routine household chores before finished.   5 4 3 2 1

19. Bursts loudly into the room when entering.   1 2 3 4 5

20. Gets very frustrated when he/she makes a mistake.   1 2 3 4 5

21. When meeting new children, acts bashful.   1 2 3 4 5

22. Stays with homework until finished.   1 2 3 4 5

23. When angry, yells or snaps at others.   1 2 3 4 5

24. Runs or jumps when going up or down stairs.   1 2 3 4 5

25. Goes back to the task at hand (chore, housework, etc.) after
    an interruption.   1 2 3 4 5

26. Moody when corrected for misbehavior.   1 2 3 4 5

27. Moves right into a new place (store, theater, playground).   5 4 3 2 1

28. Runs to get where he/she wants to go.   1 2 3 4 5

29. Responds intensely to disapproval (shouts, cries, etc.).   1 2 3 4 5

30. Has difficulty completing assignments (homework, chores, etc.).   5 4 3 2 1

31. Prefers to play with someone he/she already knows rather than
    meeting someone new.   1 2 3 4 5

32. Makes loud noises when angry (slams doors, bangs objects,
    shouts, etc.).   1 2 3 4 5

33. Gets upset when there is a change in plans.   1 2 3 4 5

34. Avoids (stays away from, doesn't talk to) new guests or visitors
    in the home.   1 2 3 4 5

35. Seems to be in a big hurry most of the time.   1 2 3 4 5

36. When an activity is difficult, gives up easily.   5 4 3 2 1

37. Has off days when he/she is moody or cranky.   1 2 3 4 5

38. Seems uncomfortable when at someone's house for the first time.   1 2 3 4 5

Page 2 of 2

Your Child's Unique Temperament: Insights and Strategies for Responsive Parenting
© 2003 by Sandee Graham McClowry. Champaign, IL: Research Press. (800) 519–2707.

Calculation Sheet

Transfer the scores from the Scoring Sheet to this sheet, then calculate an average score for each dimension by adding the values for all items in the column and dividing that sum by the total number of items.

DIMENSION	Negative reactivity	Task persistence	Approach/ withdrawal	Activity
	Items	Items	Items	Items
	2 _____	4 _____	3 _____	1 _____
	5 _____	6 _____	7 _____	13 _____
	10 _____	8 _____	9 _____	19 _____
	14 _____	11 _____	12 _____	24 _____
	17 _____	15 _____	21 _____	28 _____
	20 _____	16 _____	27 _____	35 _____
	23 _____	18 _____	31 _____	
	26 _____	22 _____	34 _____	
	29 _____	25 _____	38 _____	
	32 _____	30 _____		
	33 _____	36 _____		
	37 _____			
Sum of items				
Number of items	12	11	9	6
AVERAGE SCORE				

Your Child's Unique Temperament: Insights and Strategies for Responsive Parenting © 2003 by Sandee Graham McClowry. Champaign, IL: Research Press. (800) 519–2707.

Temperament Profile

For each dimension, compare your child's average score from the Calculation Sheet with the values given in the first and third rows of the profile:

> *If your child's score for the dimension is greater than the number in the first-row box, put an X in that box.*

> *If your child's score for the dimension is lesser than the number in the third-row box, put an X in that box.*

> *If your child's score for a dimension falls between the two numbers in the first and third-row boxes, put an X in the box in the middle row.*

NEGATIVE REACTIVITY	TASK PERSISTENCE	APPROACH/ WITHDRAWAL	ACTIVITY
HIGH	HIGH	WITHDRAWAL	HIGH
3.4	3.9	2.8	3.0
2.7	3.2	2.2	2.3
LOW	LOW	APPROACH	LOW

References

Achenbach, T. M., Howell, C. T., Quay, H. C., & Conners, C. K. (1991). National survey of problems and competencies among four- to sixteen-year-olds: Parents' reports for normative and clinical samples. *Monographs of the Society for Research in Child Development, 56* (Serial No. 225).

Baden, D. D., & Howe, G. W. (1992). Mothers' attributions and expectancies regarding their conduct-disordered children. *Journal of Abnormal Child Psychology, 20,* 467–485.

Bates, J. E. (1989). Applications of temperament concepts. In G. A. Kohnstamm, J. E. Bates, and M. K. Rothbart (Eds.), *Temperament in childhood* (pp. 321–355). Chichester, England: Wiley.

Bates, J. E. (2001). Adjustment style in childhood as a product of parenting and temperament. In T. D. Wachs & G. A. Kohnstamm (Eds.), *Temperament in context* (pp. 61–79). Mahwah, NJ: Erlbaum.

Bates, J. E., & Wachs, T. D. (1994). *Temperament: Individual differences at the interface of biology and behavior.* Washington, DC: American Psychological Association.

Baumrind, D. (1966). Effects of authoritative parental control on child behavior. *Child Development, 37,* 887–907.

Bierman, K. L., & Greenberg, M. T. (1996). Social skills training in the FAST Track Program. In R. deV Peters & R. J. McMahon, (Eds.), *Preventing childhood disorders, substance use, and delinquency* (pp. 65–89). Thousand Oaks, CA: Sage.

Block, J. (1995). A contrarian view of the five-factor approach to personality description. *Psychological Bulletin, 117,* 187–215.

Bowlby, J. (1988). *A secure base: Parent-child attachment and healthy human development.* New York: Basic Books.

Brody, G. H., Stoneman, Z., & Burke, M. (1987). Child temperaments, maternal differential behavior, and sibling relationships. *Developmental Psychology, 23,* 354–362.

Buss, A. H., & Plomin, R. (1984). *Temperament: Early developing personality traits.* New York: Wiley.

Carey, W. (with Joblow, M. M.). (1997). *Understanding your child's temperament.* New York: Macmillan.

Chess, S. (1960). Diagnosis and treatment of the hyperactive child. *New York State Journal of Medicine, 60,* 2379–2385.

Chess, S., & Thomas A. (1984). *Origins and evolution of behavior disorders.* Larchmont, NY: Brunner/Mazel.

Chess, S., & Thomas, A. (1990). The New York Longitudinal Study (NYLS): The young adult periods. *Canadian Journal of Psychiatry, 35,* 557–561.

Chess, S., & Thomas, A. (1999). *Goodness of fit: Clinical applications from infancy through adult life.* Philadelphia: Brunner/Mazel.

Collins, A. F. (1999). The enduring appeal of physiognomy: Physical appearance as a sign of temperament, character and intelligence. *History of Psychology, 2,* 251–276.

Collins, W. A., Harris, M. L., & Susman, A. (1995). Parenting during middle childhood. In M. H. Bornstein (Ed.), *Handbook of parenting: Vol. 1. Children and parenting* (pp. 65–89). Mahwah, NJ: Erlbaum.

Costa, P. T., & McCrae, R. R. (2001). A theoretical context for adult temperament. In T. D. Wachs & G. A. Kohnstamm (Eds.), *Temperament in context* (pp. 1–22). Mahwah, NJ: Erlbaum.

Cowen, E. L. (2000). Community psychology and routes to psychological wellness. In J. Rappaport & E. Seidman (Eds.), *Handbook of community psychology* (pp. 79–99). New York: Kluwer Academic/Plenum.

Eisenberg, N., & Fabes, R. A. (1999). Emotion, emotion-related regulation, and quality of socioemotional functioning. In L. Balter & C. S. Tamis-LeMonda (Eds.), *Child psychology: A handbook of contemporary issues* (pp. 318–335). Philadelphia: Psychology Press.

Eisenberg, N., Fabes, R. A., Shepard, S. A., Guthrie, I. K., Murphy, B. C., & Reiser, M. (1999). Parental reactions to children's negative emotions: Longitudinal relations to quality of children's social functioning. *Child Development, 70,* 513–534.

Elkind, D. (1967). Egocentrism in adolescence. *Child Development, 38,* 1025–1039.

Erikson, E. H. (1985). *Childhood and society* (13th ed.). New York: W. W. Norton.

Goldsmith, H. H., Buss, A. H., Plomin, R., Rothbart, M. K., Thomas, A., Chess, S., Hinde, R. A., & McCall, R. B. (1987). Roundtable: What is temperament? Four approaches. *Child Development, 58,* 505–529.

Goldsmith, H. H., Lemery, K. S., Aksan, N., & Buss, K. A. (2000). Temperament substrates of personality development. In V. J. Molfese & D. L. Molfese (Eds.), *Temperament and personality development across the life span* (pp. 1–32). Mahwah, NJ: Erlbaum.

Goldsmith, H. H., & Rieser-Danner, L. A. (1990). Assessing early temperament. In C. R. Reynolds & R. W. Kamphaus (Eds.), *Handbook of psychological and educational assessment of children* (pp. 245–278). New York: Guilford.

Goldsmith, H. H., & Rothbart, M. K. (1991). Contemporary instruments for assessing early temperament by questionnaires and in the laboratory. In J. Strelau & A. Angleitner (Eds.), *Explorations in temperament: International perspectives on theory and measurement* (pp. 249–272). New York: Plenum.

Halverson, C. F., & Deal, J. E. (2001). Temperament, change, parenting and the family context. In T. D. Wachs & G. A. Kohnstamm (Eds.), *Temperament in context* (pp. 61–79). Mahwah, NJ: Erlbaum.

Halverson, C. F., & Victor, J. B. (1976). Minor physical anomalies and problem behavior in elementary school children. *Child Development, 47,* 281–285.

Jensen, P. S., Mrazek, D., Knapp, P. K., Steinberg, L., Pfeffer, C., Schowalter, J., & Sharpiro, T. (1997). Evolution and revolution in child psychiatry: ADHD as a disorder of adaptation. *Journal of the American Academy of Child and Adolescent Psychiatry, 36,* 1672–1679.

Jouanna, J. (1999). *Hippocrates.* (M. B. DeBevoise, Trans.). Baltimore: The Johns Hopkins University Press.

Kagan, J. (1998a). Biology and the child. In W. Damon (Ed.), *Handbook of child psychology* (Vol. 3; 5th ed., pp. 177–235). New York: Wiley.

Kagan, J. (1998b). *Galen's prophecy.* Boulder, CO: Westview.

Kanner, A. D., Coyne, J. C., Schaefer, C., & Lazarus, R. S. (1981). Comparison of two modes of stress measurement: Daily hassles and uplifts versus major life events. *Journal of Behavioral Medicine, 4,* 1–39.

Kochanska, G. (1990). Maternal beliefs as long-term predictors of mother-child interaction and report. *Child Development, 61,* 1934–1943.

Kochanska, G. (1997). Multiple pathways to conscience for children with different temperaments: From toddlerhood to age 5. *Developmental Pscyhology, 33,* 228–240.

Kohnstamm, G. A., Halverson, C. F., Mervielde, I., & Havill, V. L. (Eds.). (1998). *Parental descriptions of child personality: Developmental antecedents of the Big Five?* Mahweh, NJ: Erlbaum.

Lamb, M. E., Hwang, C. P., Ketterlinus, R. D., & Fracasso, M. P. (1999). Parent-child relationships. In M. H. Bornstein & M. E. Lamb (Eds.), *Developmental psychology: An advanced textbook* (4th ed., pp. 411–450). Mahwah, NJ: Erlbaum.

Lavater, J. C. (1840). *Essays on physiognomy: Designed to promote the knowledge and love of mankind* (3rd ed., T. Holcroft, Trans.). London: Thomas Tegg. (Original work published 1775–1778)

Mangelsdorf, S. C., Schoppe, S. J., & Burr, H. (2000). The meaning of parental reports: A contextual approach to the study of temperament and behavior problems in childhood. In V. J. Molfese & D. L. Molfese (Eds.), *Temperament and personality development across the life span* (pp. 121–140). Mahweh, NJ: Erlbaum.

Martin, R. P. (1994). Child temperament and common problems in schooling: Hypotheses about causal connections. *Journal of School Psychology, 32,* 119–134.

Maslow, A. H. (1968). *Toward a psychology of being.* New York: D. Van Nostrand.

Maziade, M., Caron, C., Côté, R., Mérette, C., Bernier, H., Laplante, B., Boutin, P., & Thivierge, J. (1990). Psychiatric status of adolescents who had extreme temperaments at age 7. *American Journal of Psychiatry, 147,* 1531–1536.

McClowry, S. G. (1995a). The development of the School-Age Temperament Inventory. *Merrill-Palmer Quarterly, 41,* 271–285.

McClowry, S. G. (1995b). The influence of temperament on development during middle childhood. *Journal of Pediatric Nursing, 10,* 160–165.

McClowry, S. G. (1995c). The prevention of mental disorders in children. *Capsules and Comments in Pediatric Nursing, 1,* 13–19.

McClowry, S. G. (1998). The science and art of using temperament as the basis for intervention. *School Psychology Review, 27,* 551–563.

McClowry, S. G. (2002a). The temperament profiles of school-age children. *Journal of Pediatric Nursing 17,* 3–10.

McClowry, S. G. (2002b). Transforming temperament profile statistics into puppets and other visual media. *Journal of Pediatric Nursing, 17,* 11–17.

McClowry, S. G., & Galehouse, P. (2002). A pilot study conducted to plan a temperament-based parenting program for inner city families. *Journal of Child and Adolescent Psychiatric Mental Health Nursing, 15,* 97–105.

McClowry, S. G., Giangrande, S. K., Tommasini, N. R., Clinton, W., Foreman, N. S., Lynch, K., & Ferketich, S. L. (1994). The effects of child temperament, maternal characteristics, and family circumstances on the maladjustment of school-age children. *Research in Nursing and Health, 17,* 25–35.

McClowry, S. G., Halverson, C. F., & Sanson, A. (in press). *A re-examination of the validity and reliability of the School-Age Temperament Inventory. Nursing Research.*

McClowry, S. G., Hegvik, R. L., & Teglasi, H. (1993). An examination of the construct validity of the Middle Childhood Temperament Questionnaire. *Merrill-Palmer Quarterly, 39,* 279–293.

McClowry, S. G., Tommasini, N. R., Giangrande, S. K., Alger, M., Durand, M., Ochs, R., & Seery, V. (2000). The daily hassles of married women with children: Implications for preventive intervention. *Journal of the American Psychiatric Nurses Association, 6,* 107–111.

Merenda, P. F. (1999). Theories, models, and factor approaches to personality, temperament, and behavioral types: Postulations and measurement in the second millennium A.D. *Psychological Reports, 85,* 905–932.

Mezirow, J. (1990). Fostering critical reflection in adulthood: A guide to transformative and emancipatory learning. San Francisco: Jossey-Bass

Minuchin, S. (1974). *Families and family therapy.* Cambridge, MA: Harvard University Press.

Montagu, A. (1995). Animadversion on the development of a theory of touch. In T. M. Field (Ed.), *Touch in early development* (pp. 1–10). Mahwah, NJ: Erlbaum.

National Institutes of Health. (2000). Diagnosis and treatment of attention-deficit/hyperactivity disorder. *Journal of the American Academy of Child and Adolescent Psychiatry, 39,* 182–193.

Nunnally, J. C., & Bernstein, I. H. (1994). *Psychometric theory* (3rd ed.). New York: McGraw-Hill.

Patterson, G. R. (1982). *Coercive family process.* Eugene, OR: Castalia.

Patterson, G. R. (1983). Stress: A change agent for family process. In N. Gramezy & M. Rutter (Eds.), *Stress, coping and development in children* (pp. 133–137). New York: Appleton-Century-Crofts.

Patterson, G. R., Reid, J. B., & Dishion, T. J. (1992). *Antisocial boys.* Eugene, OR: Castalia.

Plomin, R., & Caspi, A. (1999). Behavioral genetics and personality. In L. A. Pervin & O. P. Oliver (Eds.), *Handbook of personality: Theory and research* (2nd ed., pp. 251–276). New York: Guilford.

Posner, M. I., & Rothbart, M. K. (2000). Developing mechanisms of self-regulation. *Development and Psychopathology, 12,* 427–441.

Prior, M., Sanson, A., Smart, D., & Oberklaid, F. (2000). *Pathways from infancy to adolescence: Australian Temperament Project 1983–2000.* Melbourne: Australian Institute of Family Studies.

Rappaport, J., & Seidman, E. (2000). (Eds.). *Handbook of community psychology.* New York: Kluwer Academic/Plenum.

Rothbart, M. K., & Bates, J. E. (1998). Temperament. In W. Damon (Ed.), *Handbook of child psychology* (Vol. 3; 5th ed., pp. 105–176). New York: Wiley.

Rothbart, M. K., & Derryberry, D. (1981). Development of individual differences in temperament. In M. E. Lamb & A. L. Brown (Eds.), *Advances in developmental psychology* (Vol. 1; pp. 37–86). Hillsdale, NJ: Erlbaum.

Schanberg, S. (1995). The genetic basis for touch effects. In T. M. Field (Ed.), *Touch in early development* (pp. 67–79). Mahwah, NJ: Erbaum.

Sheldon, W. H. (with Stevens, S. S.). (1942). *The varieties of temperament: A psychology of constitutional differences.* New York: Harper and Brothers.

Strelau, J. (1998). *Temperament: A psychological perspective.* New York: Plenum.

Strelau, J. (2001). The role of temperament as a moderator of stress. In T. D. Wachs & G. A. Kohnstamm (Eds.), *Temperament in context* (pp. 153–172). Mahwah, NJ: Erlbaum.

Thomas, A., & Chess, S. (1977). *Temperament and development.* New York: Brunner/Mazel.

Thomas, A., Chess, S., Birch, H. G., Hertzig, M. E., & Korn, S. (1963). *Behavioral individuality in early childhood.* New York: New York University Press.

Victor, J. B., Dent, H. E., Carter, B., Halverson, C. F., & Havill, V. L. (1998). How African American parents describe their children. In G. A. Kohnstamm, D. F. Halverson, I. Mervielde, & V. L. Havill (Eds.), *Parental descriptions of child personality: Developmental antecedents of the Big Five?* (pp. 169–187). Mahweh, NJ: Erlbaum.

Wachs, T. D. (1999). The what, why and how of temperament: A piece of the action. In L. Balter & C. S. Tamis-LeMonda (Eds.), *Child psychology: A handbook of contemporary issues* (pp. 23–44). Philadelphia: Psychology Press.

Zuckerman, M. (1995). Good and bad humors: Biochemical bases of personality and its disorders. *Psychological Science, 6,* 325–332.

About the Author

Sandee Graham McClowry, PhD, RN, FAAN, is a professor of nursing in the Division of Nursing, Steinhardt School of Education, at New York University. She received her doctorate in family nursing theory from the University of California, San Francisco, in 1988. She then did a postdoctoral fellowship at Yale University and joined the faculty there. Dr. McClowry has conducted multiple research studies in a variety of communities on children's temperament and family interactions. She was the principal investigator of the studies that tested the effectiveness of the INSIGHTS into Children's Temperament program. Dr. McClowry is a member of the American Academy of Nursing and other professional organizations and has published extensively on her research and on clinical issues, in both nursing and mental health journals.